A Week at the Beach

The Emerald Isle Travel Guide

By David L Sobotta

To everyone with memories or dreams of a beach walk on a warm summer evening under the stars along the emerald waters of the Crystal Coast

Table of Contents

First photo is looking east down the town of Emerald Isle from the Wildlife Resources Ramp. Second photo looks north at Bogue Sound from the same spot

Photos taken November 2015 by Michael Sobotta.

Introduction to 2016 Edition

We are blessed to live here on the Crystal Coast. As this book is being published just after Memorial Day in May 2016, it certainly feels like summer. We might even get our first ninety-degree day this weekend. In the week since we published the Kindle version, the skies have gone from a brilliant blue to a a lighter summer blues with puffy white clouds more typical of summer. Memorial Day brought us plenty of traffic and even a couple of bridge accidents that slowed people getting to the island. Still it was a great weekend and despite the predictions, the rains from tropical storm Bonnie missed us. As always we can hope that whenever you come, you will find great weather during your visit and that our latest version of the Emerald Isle Travel guide is useful whether you are just visiting, planning on putting down some roots here, or just dreaming.

While our print version is designed to be a companion to our Kindle version, it is also a stand-alone travel guide for much of the Crystal Coast. If you do use one of our books with the Kindle version, you will get access to extensive additional information. However, you will find it is easy to survive and have a great time on Emerald Isle with just this book

Life on the Crystal Coast is always interesting and when we find something new, we try to get it into our guides as quickly as possible so there is even some new information in this print book even though it was only published a week after the Kindle version.

This is the fourth update to our travel guide. The effort to keep current is important because the beach is an ever-changing place with businesses coming and going along with the wind and waves continually reshaping the shore. In order to make the print version more affordable, we are assuming that you have made it to Emerald Isle and the pictures and maps of the area itself are the ones that are of most value. You can get access to additional maps, specifically the ones about how to get here by buying the Kindle version. If you buy one of our paperback travel guides from Amazon, you are eligible to buy the Kindle version for only $1.99 via the Kindle matchbook program.

Most of the changes in our 2016 print version deal with new businesses or ones that have disappeared. The beach itself has not changed that much beyond some reshaping of the sands.

A beach vacation in the summer is a ritual enjoyed around the world. Our guide lets you plan time at the beach like someone who has been visiting the Emerald Isle, North Carolina area for years. With a book based on the personal experiences of locals, your vacation will be rooted in the real sand and water of the area instead of just the glossy, seductive tourist brochures. My knowledge of the area includes walking every inch of the beaches in the town of Emerald Isle and some of my friends have been here longer than me.

I have been walking the beaches of the area since 1969. I still walk some areas like the Point at Emerald Isle a couple of times a week during the warm part of the year. I usually post pictures of my hikes on Facebook in the evenings after I have had time to sort through them. If you are interested in seeing those, take advantage of the instructions at the end of the book on how to become a Facebook friend.

The Emerald Isle area is a great family beach spot with plenty of room to safely enjoy the beach without crowds. I live just a few minutes away so the perspective you will find here in this guide is that of someone who knows the area well, loves it, and appreciates being able to live here. It is not unusual for my Facebook page to even have updates of the bridge and grocery store traffic on check-in days. If you have a smartphone or cellular capable tablet, one of your passengers can keep everyone updated with what is happening in the area while you are on the road. Memorial Day Weekend you would have found me trapped in slow moving traffic on the bridge with lots of other visitors.

If a business receives a favorable mention in my guide, it is because close friends or my wife and I have used their services and been pleased. If we suggest a restaurant, it is because we had a meal that we think might be worth repeating. There is no way to buy a place in our guide. We are very open about what we know and continue to be tough about what we recommend. We make every effort to try new restaurants that open and to validate our dining experiences at longtime restaurants. When things change and it is between book updates, you will find the information on my blog or in my monthly newsletter.

Since our last edition, we have been blessed with lots of new restaurants and we will be talking about the best of them later in this book.

North Carolina has many wonderful beaches, but among all those beautiful strands of sand, the beaches along the emerald green waters of the Crystal Coast have carved a special place in the hearts of many North Carolina natives. Emerald Isle and the rest of Bogue Banks Island has long been the home beach for many North Carolina residents. After your first visit, we suspect that you will keep coming back like so many others before you. Once you sàmple our beaches and wonderful life along the coastal waters, it is hard to not come back every year.

The beaches within the town limits of Emerald Isle cover roughly eleven or twelve of the twenty-four miles of beach on the island of Bogue Banks. Other towns on the island include Salter Path, Indian Beach, Pine Knoll Shores, and Atlantic Beach.

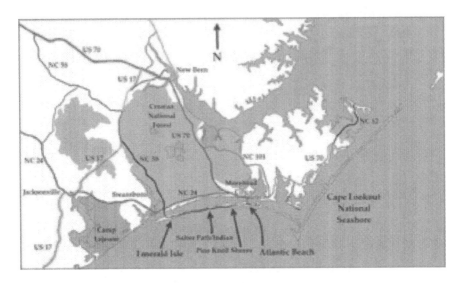

The Crystal Coast, often defined as the area from Beaufort to Emerald Isle, is part of North Carolina's Southern Outer Banks. The Southern Banks follows the coast south of Ocracoke Island and includes the Cape Lookout National Sea Shore. The Southern Outer Banks are not as well-known as the more famous and heavily visited area around Kitty Hawk and Nags Head. However, people who have visited the Southern Outer Banks will tell you that they are well worth getting to know.

One of the unique things about our beaches is that they face the south. If you are driving from Atlantic Beach on the eastern end of the island to the town of Emerald Isle at the western end around sunset, you will be driving west into the sun. The ocean water will be on your left or to the south. Bogue Sound and its waters will be to your right or to the north. It is just one of the many fun things which make the Crystal Coast a great place to spend a week at the beach and make some irreplaceable memories. There are some places along our shores where the first row on the beach is second or third row on the sound. The whole area also makes a great permanent home as many of us will attest.

The goal of this guide is to help make your stay along our beaches the most enjoyable vacation possible. As a native North Carolinian, I have been enjoying the state's beaches since shortly after my eyes were open.

I absolutely love living here. Knowing how to enjoy the area's secrets makes it one of the most rewarding places in the world to visit. A proper vacation on the Crystal Coast will bring you a greater appreciation of our natural world and let you go home with a renewed spirit. Spending time in our piece of paradise can be addictive.

The structure of the book is very simple. There is a brief section about the Crystal Coast to orient you and help validate your decision to use your precious vacation time here.

Next there are some suggestions about planning your trip and the options available in the area. We provide some general recommendations on accommodations, but because of the wide variety of available accommodations we focus mostly on the different areas that you can choose for your stay with us.

You will also get my thoughts on the best way to get here. However, the majority of the book is about what to do once you arrive. Since a lot of my enjoyment from living here comes from knowing about the birds, fish, and plant life in the area, you will find some pictures and discussion of our birds and environment in the book. I am especially fond of egrets, herons, shorebirds, and all my other woodland feathered friends, but I also love to fish so if there is a fisherman in the family, there is a chapter loaded some area fishing suggestions including savvy advice from Dr. Bogus, my good friend and the local expert on surf fishing. The Kindle version of the Week at the Beach contains a more extensive set of color pictures of birds and area waters.

There are details about other areas like Beaufort in this guide. A vacation here along the beaches of Emerald Isle is even better if you take the time to sample some of the special things in Beaufort, Morehead City, Atlantic Beach, Salter Path, and Pine Knoll Shores. If this is your first trip to the area, likely you will pick up enough tips to make the guide well worth its modest cost even if you aren't staying at Emerald Isle.

A little about the Area

First I would like to open with a message from Art Schools who served as Emerald Isle's mayor for many years until his retirement in 2013. Art was mayor for over twelve years and was instrumental in helping me put together my first travel guide back in 2012.

"In Emerald Isle, we make a sincere effort to blend together the interest of property owners (resident and non-resident), business owners, and visitors. In all of our decision making, we reflect on our goal of maintaining Emerald Isle as a "small town family friendly beach". I am really proud of the fact that many families/groups come to Emerald Isle every year for vacation and for the week or two that they are here, they feel like they are at home. The main draw for our residents and visitors is certainly the ocean, but they also are very fond of the multi-use paths, Wildlife Resources boat ramp, Emerald Isle Woods Park, fishing pier, and the other activities available in town and just across the bridge in Cape Carteret."

The team of folks in Emerald Isle work hard to make Emerald Isle one of the friendliest beach towns on the coast. I think that they do a great job and I also am grateful to Frank Rush, Emerald Isle's town manager, who provides updates each year for our guide. Now for a little about the general area.

Carteret County is 1,341 square miles in total area. If you have seen much of Carteret County or a map of the county, you will not be surprised to learn that over 60% or 821 of those square miles are water. And as many of us will tell you, that's probably a dry day at low tide. Water is a big part of life in Carteret County. The current census figures put our total population at 66,429.

The town of Emerald Isle according to the most recent numbers has 3,655 permanent residents which the town's website says makes it the fourth largest permanent beach community in North Carolina. Beaufort on the other end of the Crystal Coast has slightly over 4,000 residents. Beaufort is a wonderful waterfront spot, but it is a waterfront town with lots of boats rather than a beach town. However, beaches are easily accessible from Beaufort by boat or car.

The largest city in Carteret County is Morehead City with 8,661 people. Beyond that we have a lot of small towns which range in population from 500 to around 1,500 people. What you will find is that we have far more services than you would expect in an area with such a small population.

Emerald Isle's town website {http://www.emeraldisle-nc.org/] points out the town's low density housing. There is an average of two housing units per acre which compares to 3.4 units per acre in Carolina Beach and 4.4 housing units per acre in Kure Beach. Kill Devil Hills on the Northern Outer Banks is very similar to Emerald Isle at 1.9 units per acre.

Still in the summer time, the town of Emerald Isle can have an estimated peak population of 50,000. With that many visitors our total peak population in the summer is well over two and one half times our census population. Of course when you spread those people from one end of the county to the other, we still are not very crowded. Our most populated beach area has over twenty miles of beach, and even on a busy day there are not enough people to fill the beaches. The only time it feels crowded here is if you try to buy groceries at the Emerald Isle Food Lion on the Fourth of July weekend or if you are looking for a parking spot for the Fourth of July fireworks show.

Part of the magic of living on the Crystal Coast is that we have the 158,000 acres of the Croatan National Forest nestled by our back.

Additionally, the 57 miles of Cape Lookout National Seashore protect one flank and Camp Lejeune with the Marines holds down the other flank. If you ever get the opportunity to go a few miles north up the White Oak River beyond the railroad trestle in Stella, you will understand what I mean when I say our world is a small pocket of civilization surrounded by some lands and waters that time has not changed a lot.

Water surrounds us here in Carteret County. The White Oak River goes from being a small stream up by Maysville to being nearly two miles wide close to my home only three miles upriver from Swansboro. Bogue Sound runs behind Bogue Banks and the town of Emerald Isle. Boaters in the area know that the Intracoastal Waterway (ICW) runs through Bogue Sound down to Swansboro Harbor and beyond. It is there in Swansboro that the White Oak joins the sound. Using well-marked channels, it is easy to enjoy the water behind Bear Island or follow the ICW towards the New River. To many of us the Intracoastal is just as important as Highway 24. The ICW with its marked channel lets us go places with our boats that would be hard to visit otherwise. To me it provides a link from the White Oak River to Bogue Inlet and the wonderful fishing area just beyond the Point at Emerald Isle.

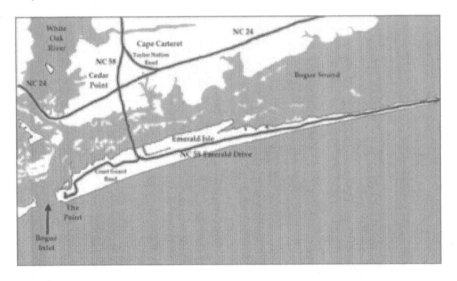

There are some other places that help define the Crystal Coast for me. One of the most special to me is the westernmost spot on Emerald Isle. It is known locally simply as the Point. You get to it by taking a right at the first stoplight as you drive onto Emerald Isle crossing the bridge from the Cedar Point-Cape Carteret area. After a short drive of 2.5 miles on Coast Guard Road you come to a stop sign. The Point is a right turn and about one third mile down Inlet drive. There you will see a vehicle access to the beach. Vehicles are not allowed on the beaches in 2016 from May 1 until September 14. On May 10, 2014, I measured 1,700 plus feet of sand west of the chain to the water. On March 11, 2016, the measurement was 1,620 feet to the water. It remains a long walk across the sand from the vehicle ramp to the actual Point. This is view from the water back to the vehicle ramp.

The Point is an extremely dynamic area and in places you get a feeling that approaches being in a truly wild spot far from civilization. The sands change dramatically depending on the weather and storms. It's one of the most stunningly beautiful areas on the North Carolina coast. It is pretty easy to put together a five-mile hike at the Point and not see it all. In November 2007, the Point was completely covered with water at high tide. Since 2012 we have been blessed with an amazing amount of sand at the Point. Sometimes when walking there, it seems you will never reach the water. However, the walk is well worth it. It is a really special treat to visit the Point after big storms like Hurricane Sandy. There are always plenty of surprises waiting.

My most recent hike at the Point was March 11, 2016 and it felt like I was visiting an old but wild friend.

Another defining element of the Crystal Coast is a town that is not officially part of it. However, if ever there was an adopted child that is well loved, it is Swansboro. The friendly waterfront town sits on the Onslow County side of the White Oak River. Swansboro is a great place that is getting even better. The always improving Municipal Park is a wonderful park for children. The 18 acres of park are accessible from Commerce Drive. The street intersects Highway 24 near Walgreens and Main Street Extension. We have spent some wonderful hours in Municipal Park with our granddaughter. Swansboro's downtown always changes a little each year. If is no surprise that 2016 has brought some new stores and restaurants along Front Street.

There is no question that the Swansboro Harbor is the gateway to some of the most beautiful marshes that I have ever seen in my well-traveled life. The area between Swansboro and Bear Island is a kayaker's paradise. The marshes form an intricate maze of pathways. The Lady Swan pontoon tour boat plies those waters out of Swansboro. Call them at (910) 325-1200 to get a ride through some of of the beautiful territory you will ever see.

Swansboro also has a second, smaller but very nice children's park, the Pirates Den Park. It is a .62-acre play area located at the junction of Broad Street and Shore Drive. You will find it just one block off NC 24. The one thing gone in 2016 is the Gazebo/pier in Centennial Park. I am sure it will be replaced.

I also have to mention the corn, soybean, and wheat fields of the Carteret County. Those crops along with the wonderful fields of produce from corn and strawberries to tomatoes and Bogue Sound watermelons keep Carteret County grounded in its rich soils. Starting sometime in June, it is possible to buy as local produce almost any vegetable you can imagine with the exception of the early spring crops which disappear with the arrival of the summer's heat. In 2016 our strawberries came early and we started enjoying them the first week in April.

There are a number of farm stands in Carteret County from Garner Farms just outside of Morehead City on Highway 70 to Winberry's on Highway 24 in Cedar Point.

Local strawberries are available until the end of May most years. Even before they were gone, the local blueberries arrive. We had a couple of boxes this year before Memorial Day. The list of summer treats seems never to end.

When you add the bounty of fresh shrimp, fish, clams and crabs that come from our waters with all that fresh locally grown produce, it is hard to disagree that the best meals are the ones you cook with the food that is grown or harvested locally. It has also become much easier to get organically raised meats and vegetables along the Crystal Coast.

We are also unique because unlike some beach areas, we have lots of vegetation along our shores. From long leaf pine trees to swamp oaks, trees, even huge bald cypresses, are well represented in the area. My favorite tree is the live oak. There are some great examples scattered all through the county. I am especially fond of the live oaks at Carteret Community College in Morehead City.

Some there and at nearby El's Drive-In and near the Carteret General hospital were damaged by a tornado during late 2013 but many survived. Pines are more prevalent over on the mainland near Emerald Isle and are often very close to the water like these near Raymond's Gut where I live.

There are some wonderful live oaks in Beaufort as you drive down Front Street and get close to the boat ramp. You will also see very nice ones on the sides of the entrance road to Hammocks Beach State Park in Onslow County. Some of my favorites are the wonderful live oaks that can be found at the beach access area at the Roosevelt Natural area in Salter Path. They are still in great shape as of the spring of 2016. There are also some beautiful live oaks at the Station Street parking lot on Coast Guard Road. I am always amazed the early settlers managed to get through our dense vegetation.

Now that you have some general information about the Crystal Coast, let us move on to the planning of the trip.

Planning Your Trip

I often tell people that the Crystal Coast is not for everyone. If your idea of a beach is a "grand strand" with high-rise condos wall to wall along a boardwalk, Emerald Isle is not the place for you. If you need more than five golf courses to be happy, you should choose some place besides Carteret County and the Crystal Coast. However, you will find free parking during the weekdays at the two large lots on Emerald Isle. That is a rare commodity at beaches these days. Even on weekends the parking is only ten dollars per day and starting this year you should be able to purchase food in the parking lot areas. Friends who live in Murrell's Inlet, South Carolina tell me that Myrtle Beach is planning to have parking meters in many areas this summer. That is also the case in Beaufort, North Carolina.

But if you love beautiful beaches, easy access to the water, and unbelievably gorgeous scenery without a lot of people, this is likely the place for you. If your idea of a great finish to a day is a night beach walk or a beautiful sunset on an un-crowded beach, you have found the right spot.

Like much of North Carolina's well-known Northern Outer Banks, most of the accommodations on the Crystal Coast are rental homes and condominiums. With just a very few exceptions, you will not find any accommodations over five stories high along the Crystal Coast. In the town of Emerald Isle there are no structures above that height.

In Emerald Isle you will find one cozy ocean front condominium operated as a hotel, The Islander. There are a very limited number of motels close by including a Best Western and the Waterway Inn, in Cedar Point. There is an almost new Hampton Inn in Swansboro and The Parkerton Inn on Highway 58 in Peletier. The Parkerton allows pets.

The vast majority of people coming to the area for a week or weekend rent either a home or condominium. The places to stay come in all sizes with everything from only the bare amenities to luxuries that are only a dream to most of us. There are a number of rental companies and at least one website with vacation rentals by owners. A good starting point is the accommodations list on the Crystal Coast tourism site. [http://www.crystalcoastnc.org/]

Make sure you check some reviews. Tripadvisor has a number of property reviews. Emerald Isle Realty provides some customer testimonials on their website. Even the Vacation Rentals By Owner site provides reviews. I can recommend one oceanfront rental where I have enjoyed the view many times. I know the owner of a special property on Heverly Drive very well and his oceanfront property has one of the best views around and is within walking distance of some of the town's restaurants and shops. Last I checked it was booked for this summer. I have always been impressed with how hard the owner works at keeping his property in great shape. Many of the places mentioned above have links to their websites in our Kindle edition if you need more information.

Read your rental contract carefully and understand exactly what you need to bring and what fees are charged. Emerald Isle Realty has a sample rental contract online. In nine summers that we have been here there have been mandatory evacuations for a couple of storms, so make certain that you understand how that will impact the money you have paid for your vacation.

We were here for Hurricane Irene. Irene made landfall about thirty miles to the east of the town of Emerald Isle. She was an impressive storm, but less than twenty-four hours later; we were having ice cream cones at the Sweet Spot on Emerald Isle. Our power was out for just under four hours. Once you see the size of the power poles running down Highway 58, you will understand. There will be more about storms and our coastal weather later. Carteret-Craven Electric Cooperative does a wonderful job of keeping electricity flowing to our homes.

In picking the spot where you will be vacationing, I can highly recommend taking advantage of aerial photos of rental homes and the beach on the websites of the rental companies. The photos can show your chosen house in relation to the beach if you do a little address research.

I like to divide the area where you can stay into just five categories. The first rental area is the heart of the town of Emerald Isle. I draw the western line to include the Pebble Beach condos and the eastern line at the municipal center that is on your left about a half-mile after the Bogue Inlet Pier stoplight. Staying in the town means that you are closer to the services in town, but you will also see a few more people. You can walk to many things if you stay in the town area. The bike paths are easily accessible.

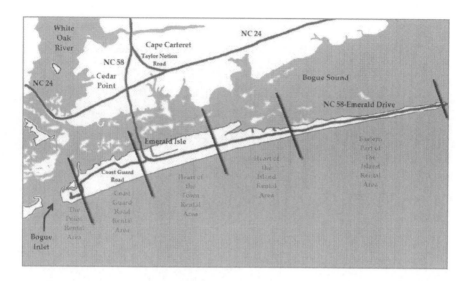

The second area is what I call the Coast Guard Road area. It runs west from the Pebble Beach condos for almost two miles to where Coast Guard Road takes a hard left and heads south towards the beach. There are a wide variety of homes in this area from modest ones to very fancy ones in Dolphin Ridge, Spinnaker's Reach and Lands End.

You can find just about anything you want in a rental in this area. The bike trail has been extended through this area. The beach is in good shape in the area, and you are also near Emerald Woods Park where I saw a great horned owl this spring. The park provides a great access to Bogue Sound including a kayak launch ramp. The accessible trail to the ramp is a boardwalk. However, the island is very wide in this area so your rental home can be a good hike to and from the beach. Make sure you check your location on a good map.

The third area is the Point. There are not as many homes available, and the beach is very wide, but there are some very popular spots along the Point. There is no better place for beach walking. Services are all back in town. However, the bike trail has made it to the Point sign where Coast Guard Road makes its final turn and heads south towards the beach.

My next section of the beaches of Emerald Isle, I call the heart of the island, and it runs for not quite two miles east from the town offices. The island is wide in this section and there are a number of sound side homes available for rent. Those homes make a great place to launch a kayak and enjoy the sound. The ocean beaches can be two thirds of a mile or more away if you rent a sound front home. There are also plenty of beachfront homes in this area. The bike trail runs through this area and all the way back into town. Again there are a wide variety of homes.

The final section of the beach is the eastern part of the town of Emerald Isle. It is the last five miles of beach before you hit Salter Path and Indian Beach. The farther east you go, the narrower the island gets. There is still plenty of sand for the beach, and there are places that you can easily get to the sound. There are also a wide variety of homes in these five miles of beach. Everything is represented from the largest of the sandcastle homes and condominiums to more modest beach cottages. It is rare to find any crowds on the beaches in this section, but you likely won't be walking to town for dinner. The bike trail has been finished to the eastern town border of Emerald Isle.

You can get a good idea of Emerald Isle and its many areas by taking my virtual tour of the town and its beaches in our Kindle edition.

There are hundreds of rentals in Emerald Isle. With so many homes used as rentals, the logistics of exiting renters being out of their homes by 10 AM and new visitors arriving a few hours later at 2 PM are challenging. Your rental week either starts on Saturday or Sunday, so things can get pretty exciting on those two days.

All these rental homes have to be freshened up in just a few short hours. Exiting renters are supposed to leave the homes clean, and mostly they do. The follow-up cleaning crews do a great job, but sometimes things get missed. Make sure you have the contact numbers that you need if you run into a problem. Usually the numbers are posted on the refrigerator. Rental owners want you to be repeat customers so most of the time problems get addressed promptly. We have spent many vacations on the coast with few problems, but I can still remember the one time in Corolla where our heat pump froze up, and the rental company could not get anyone there until the next day. We are lucky to have plenty of services in Emerald Isle and on the nearby mainland. One of the great tips for a rental home is bring as many of your beverages as possible packed in ice. If you fill an empty refrigerator with warm beverages and cold food, it will take a while before you can have a cold drink and you will have a struggling refrigerator with less than optimal conditions for your other food.

Once you have picked your home, make certain that you understand where and when you can pick up your keys. Also find out what you need to do if your trip takes longer than planned and you will be showing up outside the normal key pick up times. The traffic slowdown that we sometimes see on the two lane Emerald Isle Bridge can be impressive for those of us accustomed to going across the bridge in two or three minutes. However, I have never seen traffic in Emerald Isle that compares to traffic heading to Nags Head or across the Route 50 Bridge at the Chesapeake Bridge. Our traffic problems are tiny compared to what you can run into on Interstate 95 between Washington and Fredericksburg.

If you do not want to rent a home or stay in one of the motels there are other options. Emerald Isle is the home of the Holiday Trav-L-Park Resort which features 325 grassy sites with picnic tables, easy beach and ocean access, complete with full hookups, WI-FI available, and cable TV. They also have a pool and children's playground. I know at least one couple that bought a beach home after a stay in the Holiday Trav-L-Park. Ronnie Watson, the owner, and his team keep it in fantastic shape. It is a family business that has been around since 1976. Tammy, his daughter and owner- manager, was the first person born in Emerald Isle. They are a destination travel park and the only oceanfront camping experience on the Crystal Coast. Having visited friends using the facility, I know it is friendly, very clean, and secure. It is a great place to get to know your family. Holiday Trav-L-Park Resort is now in their 40th year and has been named one of the top 100 travel parks by the National Association of RV Parks and

Campgrounds. Holiday Trav-L-Park Resort also has a go-kart track available to the general public for a fee and an arcade with coin operated games.

If you would rather not be on the beach, there are campsites available in the Croatan National Forest at the Cedar Point recreation area. For 2016 a single site is $20 per night and a double site is $40. You can make reservations online. The Cedar Point campsite has recently been renovated. It provides great water access, some wonderful trails, and usually you can catch a glimpse of the nesting ospreys near the parking lot.

Farther up the White Oak River, there is the White Oak Shores Camping & RV Resort and in Maysville at the headwaters of the White Oak, you will find the White Oak River Campground and Fishing Lakes. I do not know anyone who has used one of these spots, but they have been in business since before we came to the area.

Now let's talk about traffic and the easiest way to arrive at your beach house in Emerald Isle either by vehicle or airplane.

Getting to the Beach

Emerald Isle benefits from being a beach destination where the density of accommodations is low and where there are multiple ways to get on the beach. You can get onto Emerald Isle from the four-lane bridge in Morehead City and drive down to the beach to the town of Emerald Isle. Driving down the beach from Morehead City can seem like a long ride at 45MPH. Or you can cross over Bogue Sound to Emerald Isle directly by following Highway 58 across the Cameron-Langston Bridge. Most of the time if you have to pick-up a key at one of the rental offices in the town of Emerald Isle, it makes sense to enter the island by Highway 58 in Cape Carteret. The map on the following gives you a basic idea of my recommended directions. The general idea is to get yourself to North Carolina 58 as efficiently as possible unless you are headed to Beaufort, Morehead City, or Atlantic Beach. If you are headed to one of those locations, stay on Highway 70 and skip Highway 58. Highway 70 continues to get better. The by-pass around Goldsboro opened last week.

I do know some of the best ways to get around North Carolina and Virginia. Based on years of monthly travel to the mountains in Virginia from the coast, I have some tried and true ways to get around the Raleigh-Durham traffic. If you need those, the best solution is our Kindle version. It has detailed directions and links to printable maps with directions in the appendix. At $1.99 with the Amazon Match Book program, our Kindle edition is cheaper than a single map. I even have some more scenic routes if you would like to avoid the interstates as much as possible. Just use the contact form on my blog to drop me a note.

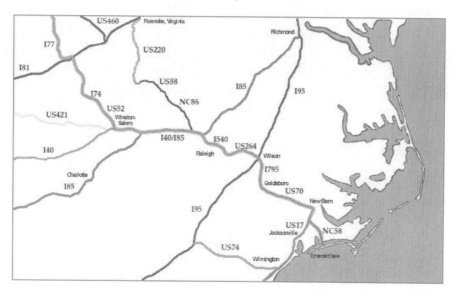

Once you are here, the biggest choke point is the intersection of Highways 24 and 58 just before the two-lane bridge to the island. This winter sunset picture will help you visualize the bridge.

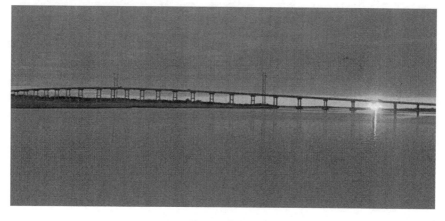

During the peak check in hours, people are often backed up the most coming from the west on Highway 24 from Swansboro. Those folks get to turn right on red, but the lane they are turning into, the right most lane, disappears within the next one quarter of a mile when you have to merge left into a single lane before crossing the bridge. People coming from the Morehead City or from the east on Highway 24 have two left turn lanes at the stoplight before the bridge. I have never seen those lanes get as backed up as the Highway 24 lanes from the west. However, all those lanes end up being one lane coming across the bridge as pictured in the next photo.

The straightest shot to Emerald Isle and the bridge goes to those people coming south on Highway 58. They have two lanes going straight, but you still have to deal with the merging into a single lane before the bridge. Obviously being in the left lane going south on Highway 58 is usually the best choice. It is a frustrating intersection.

Most of the time getting over the beach is a fairly easy proposition. Usually the best solution is just to be patient. When traffic is really bad like it was this past Memorial Day, it is almost always an accident on the bridge.

We have found that ways which bring us down Route 58 are usually the best. Jacksonville traffic can bog down quickly so you have to be careful if you really insist on traveling Highway 24 from Jacksonville to Highway 58. A new by-pass around Goldsboro opened just before Memorial Day this year so it should save time for those who choose to use Route 70 most of the way from Raleigh

If you are coming from a long distance, you might wonder which airport offers the best experience. The New Bern airport has been ranked one of the most passenger-friendly airports in the country. It is an easy drive from the airport to the Crystal Coast.

The waters waiting for you are worth the minor traffic delays you might experience getting across the bridge.

Food & Other Necessities

As you approach the bridge at Emerald Isle, there are likely some thoughts running through your head. Perhaps one of them is figuring out what you are having for dinner.

Those of us who live near the beach have learned over the years to avoid the grocery stores from early Friday afternoon until Monday morning. Friday afternoon the stores are full of homeowners coming down for the weekend. Saturday afternoon and Sunday are even worse since people moving into rentals are out shopping for dozens of people at a time.

There are plenty of grocery stores in the area but for about six weeks during the summer, they are all busy. Once people get on the island, they usually prefer not to leave that first day even though the bridge is almost never a problem later in the day. That typically means parking is at a premium in the Emerald Isle Food Lion, and the Food Lion ends up being the busiest store.

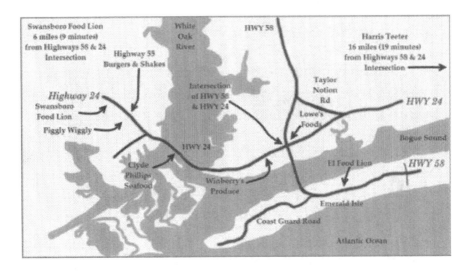

Things are not much better at the Lowe's Grocery Store on the mainland in Cape Carteret near the intersection of highways 24 and 58. It is very popular and full of shoppers on weekends in the summer.

My personal recommendation is to bring enough groceries to last through Monday's breakfast. That way when you hit the grocery store, you will miss the peak crowds. If you cannot manage to get a few groceries into your vacation vehicle, and the parking lots and crowds are too much for you at the Emerald Isle Food Lion and the Cape Carteret Lowe's, there are some options.

If you don't mind driving a little, there is another Food Lion in Swansboro less than six miles west of the mainland stoplight at routes 24 and 58. It stays busy during the week so if is only marginally better. However, if you are willing to be a little adventurous and visit one of the local favorites, try the

Piggly-Wiggly which is a couple of miles closer in Swansboro. The Piggly-Wiggly is not as fancy as the Lowe's in Cape Carteret, but we often shop there especially when the other stores are too crowded in the summer. They are good about trying to have local produce, and I am a fan of their Angus beef though the selection is not as big as it is in some of the larger stores. Piggly-Wiggly also has real butchers who will still split a chicken for you or cut you a thick steak. If you are looking for some strange part a chicken or turkey to use when going after crabs, Piggly-Wiggly probably has it and some other things you might have never imagined. All of the grocery stores can look like a swarm of locusts have been through them late on a busy Saturday or Sunday evening.

A couple of points are worth remembering if you do go shopping Saturday or Sunday evening after you have driven a few hundred miles. The grocery store parking lots are especially dangerous then since some folks have not unwound from their determined drives to the beach. Second if you decide that your shopping trip needs to be a group event, you will be compounding the crowding problem in the store. While both the local Food Lions did some remodeling a couple of years ago, their aisles can still be mighty crowded on Saturday or Sunday afternoon.

Also if you plan to go out to eat on that arrival Saturday or Sunday night, you are likely to face some long lines should you choose to eat on the island. It is especially busy at some of the more popular spots like Rucker John's or Jordan's Seafood.

When we are avoiding the crowds on beach weekends, Highway 55 Burgers and Shakes in Swansboro is often our choice. It has a table service. The burgers and menu are much better than those at the fast food chains. It is also shown on the grocery store map.

There is a Highway 55 in Emerald Plantation on the island but the mainland one which got new furniture and paint this spring is often less crowded on check-in weekends. It also has a very stable, capable crew of waitresses and cooks. It feels like the hometown eatery that it is. You will find the mainland one on the right heading west on Highway 24 in the strip mall just before you get to the Swansboro Walgreen's Drug Store. We do love and highly recommend the Highway 55 on the Island because we know the owner, Ryan, and he is often the cook. His burgers are great. When the owner cooks for you, you can count on it being good.

Do not confuse the Walgreen's in Cape Carteret by the bridge stoplight with the one in Swansboro, which is about two miles away to the west. If you stop on the light before the Highway 55 Burgers and Shakes in Swansboro, the Piggly-Wiggly is on the left also just after Walgreen's. You can have dinner and buy a few groceries afterwards without having to make two trips.

Especially on check-in nights, most of the area's best restaurants and some of the not so good ones are packed. Friday, Saturday, and even Sunday nights are the busiest. If you have been craving some Carolina fried seafood, T&Ws which is five miles north on Highway 58 from the intersection with Highway 24 can handle some very large crowds and is likely quicker than waiting to get in Jordan's on the Island. T&Ws has undergone a change in ownership and Earl has retired. T&W's even has a new paint job.

Angie's Lighthouse Café on Highway 58 in Cape Carteret is located just before the junction with Taylor Notion Road. They also serve fried seafood and are extremely popular for breakfast. Their business has grown tremendously in the last couple of years.

Another place, which is now one of my favorites is Shark's Den at the eastern end of Emerald Plantation shopping center. I love their dry rubbed wings and they also have great burger but the burgers are more expensive than the ones at Highway 55. Plaza Mexico on the Island has the best Mexican food in the area as of this spring.

Still when I am looking for fresh local fish, I go shopping at Clyde Phillips Seafood, the pink building on the water, between the bridges in Swansboro. While the building looks like it might have seen better days, you will not find fresher seafood. Buy some fresh fish and/or shrimp, and you will not be disappointed. For keeping your fish in the best possible shape until you cook it, bring a cooler with some ice and ask for ice to cover the fish or shrimp. Our Kindle version has some simple recipes in the appendix. They are great suggestions for an easy fish dinner. Flounder doesn't have to be fried to be very tasty, but it does fry very well.

I think the best seafood comes from Clyde's but some folks have a little trouble with the ambiance or the building itself that my wife continues to insist is ready to collapse. I usually reply that the building has survived many hurricanes, and I would prefer my fresh fish smelling like fresh fish instead of something else. I do sometimes buy fish from Captain Willis' in Emerald Isle, but usually his live soft shell crabs are what draw me into the shop. I brought home a couple the third week this May and fried them. They were delicious. Mostly I get my fish and shrimp either from Clyde's or Captain Sam's at Cedar Point. Captain Willis does have a larger selection of fish and regularly has salmon. Buying your fish at Clyde Phillips gives you the added advantage of seeing your fish whole before it is cleaned. Jimmy who owns Clyde's knows his fish and I never been disappointed with fish, shrimp, clams, or crab meat from there. Unfortunately, Verne one of our local icons who cleaned fish for Jimmy for years passed away this year. If you see some salmon at Clyde Phillips ask them if it is White Oak River salmon and they will likely know who sent you.

After getting your fish at Clyde's, you can get most of the produce you need at Winberry's in Cedar Point. It is on the south side or your right on Highway 24 coming from Clyde's in Swansboro and heading towards the bridge just before Redfearn's Nursery. Sarah Winberry, the owner, has the best produce in the area. Her husband, David, grows much of the produce for Sarah's stand on their farms and the land that they lease in the area. They have been doing this forever. Once again in 2016, they planted 85 acres in vegetables. No other produce stand near Emerald Isle comes close to Winberry's quality and selection. For several weeks during the summer most of what Sarah sells is all locally grown. When Sarah's produce is not on display, you can be sure its freshness is being protected in a cooler. Her corn and watermelons are hard to beat. If you want to know where some of her produce was grown, just ask. My wife and I enjoy sitting down and chatting with Sarah at her table where you will often find her making certain that everything meets her standards and keeping up with her local friends. I do not know anyone who has more of a passion for great local produce than Sarah Winberry. The next picture is a sample of what we you can find at her stand in early June.

You need to hit Clyde's and Winberry's before 6:30 PM. They both close depending on traffic between 6 and 6:30PM.

The Market at Cedar Point is now the home port of the great folks who used to run Salty-Aire Market. The Market is an open-air market with a paved parking lot and a building with refrigeration that is located on Highway 24 in Cedar Point at 1046 Cedar Point Blvd on the left going west just after Walston's Hardware. Since they have vendors who come and go, you might find something there one day and it might not be there the next. They regularly have plants, fresh fruits, vegetables, cheese, and free range grass fed meats.

If you are here on Saturday or Sunday, you might find Lil Johnny's Crab Shack, Dank Burrito or other food trucks (think barbecue) operating there. Little Caesar's Pizza has announced they will in the parking lot by the Market with their hot and ready truck on Thursday evenings. You will also find lots of crafts and fresh seafood there on the weekends.

We also have a good selection of brick and mortar pizza places including three Michaelangelo's locations, a Domino's, a Papa John's, and Emerald Isle's Circle Pizza which we have never tried. While it won't help you on check-in weekends, from Monday through Thursday we enjoy the large three topping pick-up special at $7.99 from the Domino's in Cedar Point. I usually order it using the Domino's app on my smartphone and it is ready by the time I arrive. You can also get fried chicken, barbecue, or fried seafood at Bogue House in Cedar Point. Bogue House does serve some local vegetables, but be prepared to eat on Styrofoam. Their collards are tasty but not in same class as the ones cooked by Miss Jan for our monthly church luncheons during collard season. The Cedar Point Grille in the BP Station on the right headed towards Swansboro just after the Quality Inn does some excellent fried chicken tenders.

Once you make it through the first night of food and that first early morning beach walk, you might be interested in going out for breakfast especially if you still haven't gotten any groceries. There are getting to be more choices for breakfast in the area. The old favorites were Yana's in Swansboro and

Mike's on the Island. Mike's is gone and the real breakfast traffic seems to have moved to Angie's Lighthouse and Carteret Café. Both can be crowded on the weekend so go early or expect to wait. This map shows the places we have eaten meals over the years and been satisfied with the food and service.

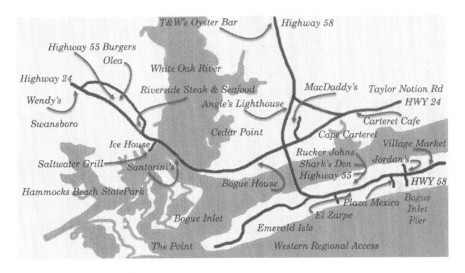

My map also has what I call the three fried fish spots, Jordan's, T&W's, and Bogue House. We have "mostly" given up on deep fried fish and oysters but even we fall off the wagon once in a while. If you want Carolina fried fish, you will likely be happy with what you find in any of the three restaurants. However, it is getting harder and harder to get good fried fish. Fresh fish prices continue to rise faster than almost anything else and if you want local fish, the best guarantee is to cook it yourself. If you are on the island and end up in a very long line at Jordan's, you might want to consider driving to T&W's just north up Highway 58. The drive is under fifteen minutes. T&W's is a bigger restaurant but they also get very busy and they are under new ownership so we have not checked them out since Earl left.

When it comes to lunch, our favorite spot used to be Mike's on Emerald Isle. Mike has retired and the restaurant has undergone a huge renovation and a change in appearance which is hard to believe but the above picture provides a good idea of the changes. As of early June 2016, it is still not open. The rumor is that the new restaurant will be called the Trading Post. It is supposed to be open for breakfast, lunch, and dinner. Lunch will be Southern style food and dinner will be seafood focused. If we can get in it this summer, we will try it.

The Village Market, which expanded a few years ago is located in the same building as the Reel Outdoors, also has good food. They have very nice sandwiches and beautiful desserts. We have not tried their breakfast, but the dining area is very pleasant and we have enjoyed eating quick sandwiches there several times. They also have some outdoor seating. Chowdaheads which was across the street is now closed and up for sale.

One of the most pleasant places to eat in the area is Ribeye's near the intersection of Highways 24 & 58. It has a very nice salad bar and is one of our favorite spots for a quiet lunch. They have fairly flexible seating so a family has a good chance of getting a table. In Swansboro, you will find The Boro, which does smaller meals. They have completely remodeled. The interior is beautiful and in addition to sandwiches they have lots of delicious sweets. They are connected to The Ice House, which we also enjoy for lunch on the water.

El Zarape is dependable for a basic Mexican meal, but I have found that I really enjoy Plaza Mexico on 140 Fairview Dr. in Emerald Isle. I especially enjoy the guacamole that they make right at the table. Plaza Mexico is on the road just before the turn to Bogue Inlet Pier. Shark's Den in Emerald Plantation has also turned into a real favorite of ours. I find their dry rubbed wings nearly perfect. It is also a very pleasant place to eat. At least during lunch and the early evening hours, it is not nearly as noisy as some sports bars. We enjoy grabbing a table where we can look out at the live oaks in the parking lot.

Another new area restaurant, Santorini's Mediterranean Grill, has become one of our go-to places in Swansboro. Their gyro platter with Greek salad and house dressing is a favorite of mine. My wife really enjoys their chicken Souvlaki. I also like their calamari. My son claims some of their Greek appetizers are as good as they come. They have a deck where you can eat by the water and look across the Intracoastal Waterway. Santorini's also has online ordering and you can even pay for your meal with Android Pay. They get very busy during the summer. Below is a picture of my favorite gyro platter lunch at Santorini's.

We also have another new restaurant, Olea Mediterranean Kitchen in Swansboro by the Post Office. I have not found anything that I did not like there and they have great desserts. Seaside Coney Island at 632 W Corbett Ave, Swansboro, is a nice friendly burger and hot dog place. The BP Grill in Cedar Point at 605 Cedar Point Blvd in Cedar Point has great fried chicken tenders but the service can be slow if they are understaffed.

Swansboro, Cedar Point, and Cape Carteret have most of the fast food places covered. Wendy's is the farthest at 809 W

Corbett Ave in Swansboro, but it is still less than five miles or seven minutes from the stoplight in Cape Carteret at Highways 24 & 58. The Subway in Cape Carteret is reliable and if Chinese food is your thing, Golden China near Lowes Grocery Store does good takeout food. I like their General's Chicken. Their phone number is (252) 393-3888.

Subscribing to my newsletter [https://about.me/dsobotta] is one of the best ways to receive updates on all the restaurants in the area. We mention restaurants and good meals during the year as we dine out.

If you are looking for a special meal in the area and want it to be some of the best seafood that you have ever eaten, I can highly recommend the grouper at Riverside Steak and Seafood in Swansboro. I think Riverside is consistently the best restaurant in the area. Their prices have risen some over the years but their serving sizes are still good. While it probably does not need emphasis, I love their grouper. In the section about the Beaufort area, I will mention some additional restaurants, which are also consistently good.

One of the really good things about North Carolina is that restaurant sanitation grades have to be conspicuously posted. We tend to turn around and walk out if any restaurant has a grade lower than 90 or 92. Most of our area restaurants are either family operations or small regional chains. They can get overwhelmed with customers during the summer rush so be patient and understand that the food is highly dependent on the chef cooking that day.

Check out some of the standard online recommendations and reviews before you eat in a place if I have not mentioned the restaurant. Like everywhere, a nice view or years in business does not guarantee good food. As a general rule for restaurants in the area, go early for breakfast, late for lunch and early for dinner especially on the island. A new rooftop restaurant is supposed to open in Emerald Isle this summer, and we will try it when it opens.

One of the things we have done when traveling about the area is to take a cooler with some ice. Some things travel well but few things can survive a hot car in the summer time without ice. If you are willing to travel a little I can highly recommend Fat Fellas in Newport. Their fried chicken and barbecue combo is under nine dollars and is enough food for two meals. I love their butter beans. Surprisingly you can get to Fat Fellas in Newport from the bridge stoplight in Cape Carteret in twenty-one minutes, a little quicker than you can make it to Smithfield's Chicken and Barbecue in Morehead City. You will find less traffic on the way to Newport than Morehead City.

To reach Fat Fellas take a right at the 24 and 58 stoplight after crossing the bridge from Emerald Isle. Follow NC 24E for 10.8 miles. Turn left on Hibbs Road and stay on it for 3.7 miles. Turn right on Roberts Rd and shortly after that turn left on East Chatham St. In a little over six tenths of a mile Fat Fellas is on your right. I know folks who claim this is the most authentic Eastern Carolina barbecue in the area.

When you leave Fat Fellas, it is easy to go east on Highway 70 and hit all the shopping spots including Harris Teeter in Morehead City. Whichever barbecue or fried chicken you choose, if you need it for a later meal, it does travel well in a cooler.

Lowe's Foods in Cape Carteret also sells tasty fried chicken and often has it on special. Morehead City has most of the national chains including a Panera and even a Starbucks. Morehead got a Longhorn Steakhouse a few years ago and an iHOP to go along with their Five Guys and Buffalo Wild Wings. You can easily be in Morehead City in less than twenty minutes from the intersection of Highways 24 and 58. Jacksonville has even more places but is plagued by traffic which means it takes longer to get there and to move from one end of town to the other even with the new roads.

One of the places that we really enjoy in Morehead City is Banks Grill. They have a great breakfast and I think they have the best shrimp burger in the area. They get their shrimp locally in Harker's Island. My wife enjoyed flounder tacos there recently. Banks Grill does close at 2PM so keep that in mind. On our list to try in Morehead City is Southern Bread Bakery & Café. We have heard good things about them.

If you are in Morehead City early on a Saturday morning try the curbside market corner of 13th and Evans St, downtown Morehead City; Saturdays from 7:30 - 11:30 am. They have local vegetables and goodies. Say hi to my good friends Vera and Dave who often sell day lily roots and plants there.

There are Bojangles locations in Morehead City and Atlantic Beach if a Hardee's or McDonald's biscuit will not do. The Pita Plate is in the shopping center not far from Hobby Lobby. If you want sweets and Dunkin Donuts in Cedar Point does not cure your cravings, there is a new donut place on the road to Bogue Inlet Pier. I brought home a killer donut twister thing the day that I took the picture.

We also have a couple of cupcake places, Happycakes Cupcakery in Morehead City and Frosted in Swansboro. I lean a little towards Happycakes but I eat cupcakes maybe once a year so I am no expert. Either one will overload your senses.

Fun Things to Do

With shelter and food taken care of, it is time to start thinking about doing some fun things. You are at the beach so certainly it will be a big part of your vacation. If you like to do more than roast yourself on the beach, I have a few suggestions.

First off, beach walking is very popular on Emerald Isle. Some folks just walk and others pick up shells along the way. I walk and take pictures, and sometimes do it with a fishing rod in my hand. It is possible to see all of the beaches inside the town limits of Emerald Isle by foot. I have done all of the beaches at least twice some summers, and every summer I do my favorite spots multiple times.

If you are a serious beach walker, learn to pay attention to the tides. My favorite time to walk is an hour or two before low tide. The beach is generally best for walking on a falling tide. A rising tide usually fluffs the sand a little and makes for harder walking. Beach walks early in the morning and later in the evening are my favorites.

Most beach houses are within walking distance of one of the marked Coastal Area Management Authority (CAMA) paths that provide public access to the beaches. If for some reason, you are not within walking distance of one of those, there are some options. First of all, there are two large regional-access parking areas inside the town limits of Emerald Isle. The Western Regional Access is just off Islander Drive which is the first right after the first stop light on Emerald Isle after you cross the bridge from Cape Carteret. Just follow the signs as you get close to the water.

When you arrive you will find a large paved parking lot with 168 spots, changing rooms, bathrooms, showers, picnic shelter, and a couple of beach volleyball courts. It also has a ramp to the beach so you can use one of the special beach wheelchairs that are available free on a first come, first served basis at the main Emerald Isle Fire Department. There are also concerts at this beach access. In 2016 the EmeraldFest Concerts start at 6:30PM on Thursday, June 16, and run through August 18. Many businesses in the area have posters with the EmeraldFest artists and dates listed. The two regional parking areas will also have rotating food vendors on selected days during the 2016 beach season. Swansboro has SwanFest concerts at 6:30 PM on Sunday evenings in their pavillion. They started this year on May 15, and run through September 18. You can pick schedules for both EmeraldFest and SwanFest at the two local travel bureaus or I have links to them in my Kindle edition.

The second regional access, the Eastern Regional Access, is about six miles east up the beach from the intersection of Highway 58 and Coast Guard Road. It now has a paved parking lot, and there are 250 parking spaces, changing rooms and bathrooms along with a nice access to the beach including a wheelchair ramp. From April 1 to September 30, parking at one of the regional accesses costs $10 per day on Saturday, Sunday, and holidays from 7 AM to 4 PM. The Eastern Regional Access will be the spot if Emerald Isle eventually moves head with their plans to build a new concrete pier. That is not on the horizon at this point.

The parking fee provides for lifeguards and for a better-funded effort to keep the beach, restrooms and changing rooms in great shape for visitors. This year, 2016, brings the first attempt at having rotating food vendors available at the regional accesses.

There are Lifeguards on duty from 10 AM to 5:00 PM every day of the summer at both regional access areas. You will find the protected areas clearly marked. There are also two mobile trained lifeguards patrolling the town's 12 miles of beaches during the same hours.

People visiting by car for the day use mostly the two regional beach accesses. Very little of the town of Emerald is not within walking distance of a beach. However, even paradise is better with the spice of variety. There is nothing wrong with exploring some of the other beaches instead of staying on the one near your beach home. In the summertime I either go to the beach very early in the morning or after 4 PM. Most of the time, with very busy weekends and the Fourth of July weekend being the exceptions, I do not have any trouble finding a parking spot in my two favorite beach accesses. My absolute favorite place for a beach hike as I mentioned earlier is the Point area that is down the Coast Guard Road.

For a beach hike at the Point, follow these directions. Turn right onto Coast Guard Road at the first stoplight as you cross over to the island. If you are leaving the island, it is the last stoplight, and you will make a left turn. Follow Coast Guard Road 2.4 miles, and you will see the small, sixteen space Station Street Parking lot on your right. The town built a bike path down Coast Guard Road during spring of 2014. They also extended the bike path to the east up the beach to the town limits of Emerald Isle. The bike path is a tremendous asset for homeowners and visitors and has a total length of eleven miles.

If you want a parking space for a Point hike in the summer, it is good to be there fairly early in the morning or when the morning crowd starts leaving in the afternoon. There is no bathroom available so keep that in mind. After parking you can reach a CAMA beach access point either by walking left on Station Street and then left on Channel Drive or go right on Coast Guard Road and then left or right at the stop sign on Wyndtree Drive.

Both access points are roughly two tenths of a mile away. The only difference is that the Station Street route puts you further west and a little closer to the Point. Even when you get to the CAMA access points, there is still a little hike of around 800 feet or nearly three football fields to actually get to the water. You will find that there is a lot of sand in the area close to the Point. On May 5, 2014, I measured the distance from the vehicle ramp at the end of Inlet Drive to the edge of the water in Bogue Inlet just across from Bear Island. It was very close to one third of a mile. That is over 300 feet more sand than I measured in October 2013.

You can just about walk your legs off at the Point. A walk I did there on March 16, 2013 was 3.7 miles and I used a short cut back to the car. A hike in April 2013, where I stayed on the beach as much as possible the hike was 4.2 miles. If you park at the Station Street lot and go on the beach at the access access along Inlet Drive and then walk down the beach until you are directly opposite the vehicle access point on Inlet Drive and head back to the Station Street lot, you will have a hike of about 1.75 miles like the one that I did in the spring of

2016. If you take a left where Coast Guard Road ends and walk east along Wyndtree Drive and take that beach access and head west towards the Point, your hike will be about two miles like this one. That seems to be my favorite hike.

Sometimes you see some amazing birds at the Point like these Red Knots who are long distance champions traveling 9,000 miles from the Artic to the southern tip of South America.

Based on Google's maps I sometimes wonder if I have the ability to walk on water. The truth is that the Point changes faster that the aerial photographs. My track is along the beach and is very accurate. There are some maps of hikes on the coming pages

The following picture, is one of my favorites of the Point. It is looking south towards Cedar Point from the northernmost part of the Point. Of course it does not look like that today. The small body of water was gone even in 2014. The way the Point changes it might be back later this summer.

The next picture is a map created using my smartphone and Google MyTracks. The two hikes were done on October 3, 2013 and on May 5, 2014, roughly seven months later. The distance from water to ramp in May 2014 was very close to one third mile. That is approximately 317 additional feet of sand. The hikes were at roughly same tide and I was not doing any walking on water. Change in the outline of the Point becomes very obvious in a couple of years.

By comparing the map above with the one below from a March 2016 hike, it is easy to see how the Point has changed in just a few years. Fortunately, Google has taken some new base map pictures so I do not appear to be walking on water these days.

The Point is an exceptionally fascinating place to many of us residents. Certainly the sand is far different than what is shown on some of the earlier Google base maps.

My other favorite beach hiking access place is the Third Street Beach. With a starting point of the Coast Guard Road stoplight on Emerald Drive just after you cross the bridge head 8.4 miles east. Stay on Emerald Drive until you get to Fifth Street. Take a right and then an immediate left, and you will see the small twelve-car parking lot on your right after a short drive.

The beach is a very short walk from the parking lot. There is no bathroom and actually there is no Third Street either. The beach is just named Third Street. There is a ramp to the observation deck and picnic table, but there are only steps from that down to the beach. Even with that, this is a good beach for fishing since you don't have to haul your gear very far, and there are some good places to fish just west of the beach access. There is a pronounced off shore sand bar, and fish often cruise between it and the shore. Cuts through the sandbar are especially productive.

Third Street is also a good place to try your beach hiking legs. If you walk out on the beach and take a right, you will find the space-ship-shaped Bogue Banks Water Tower about one half mile west. If you walk down to the water tower and back, you will have chalked up your first mile of walking on the beach. Do not forget that beach walking is easier on a falling tide, just an hour or two before low tide.

There are a number of individual handicap parking spots at beach access points within the town of Emerald Isle. There are a couple on Inlet Drive but there is no ramp to the beach. Both Eastern and Western Regional Accesses have accessible beach access with ramps. There is a list parking places at the town website.

Some of my other favorite beach access points with parking are actually not inside the town limits of Emerald Isle. About 10.5 miles down the beach from the Coast Guard Road stoplight, you will find a very nice beach access in the Roosevelt Natural Area. There are plenty of shaded parking spaces, a bathroom and outside showers. The elevated boardwalk to the beach is very special as it winds its way through and under a canopy of natural vegetation and then drops down steeply through a set of steps to the beach.

A note of caution, the speed limit drops to 35 MPH once you enter Salter Path. We have eaten good seafood at The Crab Shack. I have had whole fried clams there but it has been a while since I visited. They have had steamed blue crabs in the past. The Big Oak Barbecue also provides good sandwiches. Frost Seafood is now Bogue Banks Seafood but we have not tried it.

The last beach access to keep in mind is the one at the Iron Steamer in Pine Knoll Shores. It is on the right 13.5 miles from the Coast Guard Road stoplight. There are bathrooms and a nice parking lot with easy access to the beach.

I mention these beaches further down the beach from the town of Emerald Isle because if you are making one of the day trips I suggest, sometimes with children it helps to have a stop where everyone can run on the beach for a few minutes after being cooped up in the car. Having bathrooms along the way is also helpful.

There is plenty of beach sand to enjoy in Emerald Isle, but another favorite beach of mine is just across the river in Onslow County. It is a great opportunity to combine an inexpensive boat ride with an afternoon or morning at the beach.

For those who do not have access to a boat while vacationing in the area, a visit to Hammocks Beach State Park gives you the chance to take a boat ride through our beautiful marshes and to spend some time on one of the nicest beaches in the area.

The Hammocks Beach State Park is located at the end of Hammocks Beach Road. You can get there with these directions. To reach the park head across the bridge then west on Highway 24 through Swansboro. Turn left at the new Hampton Inn on Old Hammocks Beach Road. When it intersects Hammocks Beach Road by the new Catholic Church take a left. The entrance to the park is on the right a little over eight tenths of a mile after you make the turn.

Call the park at (910) 326-4881 before you go to check schedules and pricing. The last time I was there, the pontoon boat ferries ran every thirty minutes. An adult, thirteen and over, round trip ticket costs five dollars. It you are 62 and older, the ticket is three dollars and if you are six to twelve, the ticket is also $3. Under six you get a free ticket as long as you are with an adult. The full summer schedule starts on May 28 this year. Most days the ferry runs every thirty minutes from 9:30 AM to 5:30 PM but it is best to check before you go. You buy your ticket inside, and if you want to kill some time there is a nice small free museum and of course bathrooms. The park also has a wonderful kayak launch point.

Once you get on the very safe, covered pontoon boat, you will have a scenic ride of about three miles from the ferry terminal just off Queens Creek, down the Intracoastal Waterway, and out Cow Channel to Bear Island, the location of the park's beaches. The ride takes about twenty minutes each way.

Once you dock on the north side of Bear Island, you will see a small covered pavilion that is a perfect waiting spot for the ferry after a long day at the beach. The walk from the dock to the south side of the island where the beach is located is about one half mile. It is a single lane paved road. It is an easy twelve to fifteen-minute walk to the beach from the dock.

Once you get on the other side of the island, there are two large pavilions that have bathrooms and places to change clothes. There is a small snack bar that sells bottled drinks, chips, and candy bars. The walkways between the two pavilions also have a number of nice covered picnic tables.

The beach has lifeguards and is wide, beautiful, and uncrowded. There are also campsites that you can register to use and there are showers for the campers. A day at Hammocks Beach State Park is one that your family will remember forever. The beaches are as beautiful as they get.

When using any beach, everyone needs to be mindful that the ocean is not a swimming pool. There are strong currents by times, and there are no lifeguards except at the regional accesses and Hammock's beach during the warmer months.

The beach is a good spot for common sense. Being smart at the beach starts with no one going into the water alone unless they are in water that is only knee deep. Even at that shallow depth young children need an adult with them. The ocean can easily best strong swimmers. Sometimes floats can actually get you in more trouble than wading as it is easier for a current to catch you when you are on a float than it is when you are standing with your feet in the sand.

You also need to watch for soft sand. Sometimes water draining from the beach can create very soft sand. I stepped into this very innocent looking spot and got one foot stuck. I am sure I was an interesting sight, balancing myself one foot while trying to extricate my foot and keep from falling into the water which would not have been good for my camera. I have probably stepped in the water at that spot along the south side of the Point dozens of times without problems.

Where I got stuck

While my children were teenagers, I spent a lot of time jumping waves with them. I am not sure they were happy with me even though I tried to stay in the background, but none of my children ever got into trouble in the ocean so I would do it again without any hesitation. We made some great memories out in the waves.

Children are not the only ones who face challenges at the beach. If your dog is not used to being outside, the beach can be very stressful. Make sure the family pet gets plenty of shade, water, and some serious napping time in the air conditioning during the worst heat of the day.

Just a little caution can make those days on the beach nearly perfect. Don't leave anything on the beach after dark that you do not want the beach patrol to haul off. There are bins for trash conveniently located at CAMA access points. Also pets are supposed to be on leash at all times. I see them off leash in remote areas, but I do not think the beach patrol is happy about it if they see your dog running free. Please remember to keep our beaches clean from any animal waste.

If your young children get bored of the beach, there is a wonderful new accessible playground that just opened by the Emerald Isle boat ramp.

Beyond beach walks and jumping waves, there are times when we get plenty of wind for some nice east coast surfing, wind surfing, and just playing with kites. We have more wind in the spring but we can get a nice breeze at any time especially when a storm sneaks up the coast.

This next picture of someone riding the waves was taken on May 20, 2014 near the Roosevelt Natural Area in Salter Path.

Storms especially when they are just off shore can bring some great waves for surfing.

With all this physical outdoor activity, one of things that you might enjoy a good massage, I can recommend Wellness Massage by Byrns & McCormick. They are licensed, located in Emerald Isle and work by appointment only, so call 252 240-9296.

If you are here long enough, you might want to try some of the traditional beach activities such as Putt-Putt which the whole family can enjoy. The Golfin'Dolpin also home of Mac Daddy's has everything you need from a Putt-Putt course to Go-Karts, Bumper Boats, and Water Wars. If you turn left from Highway 24 at the Cape Carteret Walgreen's and just keep going, you will soon arrive at MacDaddy's.

If you need even more physical activity and cannot find enough outside, you might want to try the Aquatic and Wellness Center located on Taylor Notion Road in Cape Carteret. You can get a daily pass for $12 with a temporary membership.

Of course for any extended time on the beach or out in the sun, do not forget some water, hats, sunglasses, and sunblock. If you are walking at night watch for turtles and please be careful around the nests. Try to keep your outside lighting at a minimum if you have an oceanfront home. Bright lights can distract the young turtles when they are making their way into the ocean

Kayaking, A Favorite Activity in the Area

If you need more than beaches in your vacation, there is plenty to do in the Emerald Isle area. If you love the water, there is an abundance of activities beyond relaxing on the beach or trying to hike to the bottle trees.

One of the favorite things to do in the area is kayaking. There are a number of places where you can rent kayaks in the area. One of the popular spots is Barrier Island Kayaks in Cedar Point right beside the Waterway Inn. They also offer the standup paddleboards. Barrier Island Kayaks is just off the Intracoastal Waterway. Their location offers easy access to the marshes between Swansboro and Bear Island and the White Oak River. The following map is a boat trip from our house on Raymond's Gut just off the White Oak River down to Swansboro, east on the Intracoastal Waterway and out the channel to the Point. From there we made our way back behind Bear Island (Hammocks Beach State Park) and then followed Cow Channel back to the Intracoastal Waterway which took us back to Swansboro. The area surrounded by the lines of our boat trip are some of the best kayaking waters around.

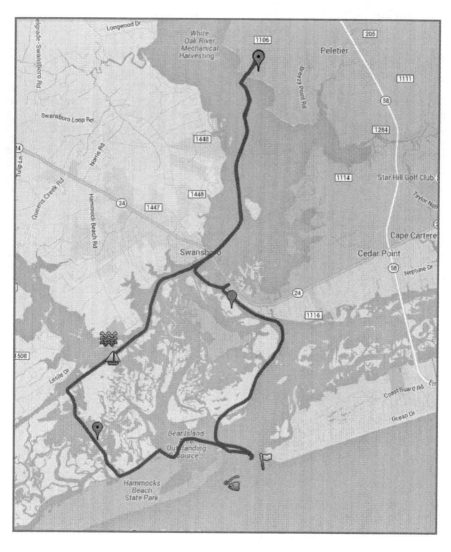

The following picture shows kayaks just behind Barrier Island Kayaks just off the Intracoastal in Cedar Point.

Second Wind Eco Tours and Yoga is located in Swansboro. You can do some kayaking out to Bear Island and top it off with yoga and breakfast. Another popular option is Flatwaters Paddling in Emerald Isle. They specialize in standup paddle boards which are definitely not kayaks but certainly another way to get out on the water. PaddleNC also offers rentals with the trips based out of nearby Hammocks Beach State Park.

The West Channel, which goes from just across the ICW at Swansboro Harbor along the marshes and then on the north side of Huggins Island, is a beautiful spot to get a taste of kayaking. I often see bottle nosed dolphins swimming in there when I go for my early morning fishing trips. It would not be unusual to see my 20 feet long Sundance skiff in there before 8 AM on a summer morning.

If you have your own kayak, there are even more great places to launch. One of the nicest launch points is the shore side part of Hammocks Beach State Park. They have a beautiful kayak launch point, and there is plenty of great water to explore in the area that is at the mouth of Queen's Creek. There is even a kayak trail over to Bear Island and PaddleNC offers rentals of kayaks and canoes right by the launch point. Call ahead at 910-612-3297 or get a discount for reserving online.

Hammocks Beach has a very nice setup, which includes two kayak ramps. My last visit they had one ramp (not pictured) adjusted for launching and the other set for getting out of the water. There is also a new launch point at Centennial Park in

Swansboro by the bridges. Sometimes folks will launch from the grass at the edge of the parking lot at the Wildlife Resources Ramp in Cedar Point and there is a new kayak launch Point at the end of the main trail in Emerald Woods.

To get to Hammocks Beach State Park follow these directions. Head across the EI bridge back to the mainland, take a left on Highway 24 west and keep going through Swansboro until you see the new Hampton Inn on your left. Turn left there on the Old Hammocks Beach Road and in about a mile you will run into Hammocks Beach Road. Turn left there and watch for the signs to the park entrance. The total drive is about 8.5 miles.

A favorite spot for many fishermen using kayaks is the Croatan National Forest access in Cedar Point. The marshes around the launch point are good places to fish for red drum. Launching at the Croatan Trail access can take you into the White Oak River, which is an impressive coastal river. Paddling over to Jones Island that is visible from Highway 24 in Swansboro is a nice morning paddle. The Croatan launch point is a boat ramp suitable mostly for smaller boats but it is only four miles from the intersection of Coast Guard Road and Emerald Drive. You will make a left onto VFW Road 2.7 miles from the Coast Guard Road intersection. Next turn left onto the National Forest access road in about one half mile.

Be careful when launching from any boat ramp. The ramps can be slippery. I always try to find a grassy or sandy spot to launch my kayak.

If paddling in a river that is one to two miles wide like the White Oak makes you nervous, you can head up to Stella about 12.5 miles from the island and launch your kayak at Boondocks where the river is much narrower. There is a fee for the launch point and parking.

The river above the railroad trestle is far deeper with much more current, but the river is very different and uniquely scenic at that point. It can be very difficult paddling against the current. Upriver from Stella you are in wild country with almost no humans on the edge of the river after the first few minutes of paddling.

If you want to just cruise with the current and have a couple of vehicles to work with, you can put in at Haywood Landing off Highway 58 and take your kayak out at Boondocks.

Good maps of the White Oak and the Bogue Sound area are available at Dudley's Marina in Cedar Point and Reel Outdoors in Emerald Isle.

The White Oak River on a particularly beautiful day.

Hiking Beyond the Beach

There are lots of woods interspersed with our sandy beaches. Fortunately, great trails seem to go along with all those wooded areas.

My two favorite trail areas are very easy to reach. The best trails in the area are those located at the Croatan National Forest access point in Cedar Point. They are easy to find. Follow these directions from the mainland. Starting at the intersection of Highways 24 and 58 in Cape Carteret, go seven tenths of a mile north on Highway 58 and turn left on VFW Road. It is the first left north of the stoplight. Drive one half mile and turn left at the sign announcing the Croatan National Forest. It is about eight tenths of a mile after you turn left until you reach the trailhead.

You will find a map at the trailhead. There is a short loop trail, which takes you to a nice bay of the White Oak River. You will find a convenient bench there for watching the action on the water. I have seen some snowy egrets and juvenile ibises while enjoying the bench.

The only caution is to watch for poison ivy off the edge of the trail during the summer. If you have a dog and they wander into the poison ivy, you can get it from petting your dog.

However, do not let a little poison ivy off the edge of the trail scare you away. The trails are exceptionally well maintained and a wonderful way to see some of the Croatan National Forest. The Big Loop trail is a great mix of marshes and forests. The Cedar Point Access also has a restroom, small pier, small boat ramp and picnic tables near the parking area. The trails are not far from a large camping area. We enjoy watching the ospreys that nest in the area. This year their nest is easily visible from the parking area. The next picture is of one of the bridges across the marshes at the Cedar Point trails.

If you want an even more convenient trail, it is really hard to beat Emerald Woods. Follow these directions. Make a turn onto Coast Guard Road from Emerald Drive. Just a hair over one half mile down Coast Guard Road you will find the entrance to the Emerald Woods Park. The parking lot for the trail is not quite one quarter of a mile down a graveled road. A little farther down the road is a drop off point and some accessible parking. It is a very easy trail and one that is accessible with wheelchairs.

It is a beautiful walk through the woods to Bogue Sound. If you know where to look and are not driving, it is easy to spot the Emerald Woods' dock from the bridge to Emerald Isle.

As I mentioned earlier there is now a kayak launch point at the floating dock at the end of the trail. The trail since it is all boardwalk before the floating dock is suitable for a kayak cart.

The floating pier is a great place to watch sunsets but if you want to sit there and enjoy it with someone special, arrive early because I often see couples there as the sun starts to fade.

There are also bathrooms at the park.

Taking to the water in something besides a Kayak

Those of us who live here on the Crystal Coast do suffer from being singularly focused on the water so it should be no surprise that I strongly recommend that you take the time to go boating so you can truly appreciate the beauty of the area from the water.

Of course boating works best if you have your own boat. It is possible to rent a boat but it is not very common. Some fishermen hire a guide with a boat. You can get current recommendations for guides with boats at Reel Outdoors, Dudley's Marina or Casper's Marina. If you do have your own boat, be aware that the waters in our area have been described as an awful lot of water spread mighty thin across some very shallow marshes and inlets. The warning I got when I first started boating here has proved true. It is not if you will get stuck on a sandbar, it is when. Just remember that it is a lot easier to unstick a boat that goes aground at speeds less than 30MPH. I speak from experience.

Boating along the Crystal Coast is not like boating on a lake. If you are planning on boating here, it really helps if you have taken the Coast Guard Auxiliary boating course, America's Boating Course. This is a very safe area where it is easy to enjoy the area's waters but to be safe you must understand how to read marked channels and it is critical that you pay attention to the tides. I could tell you the golden rule of "Red on the right" returning, but this is not a boating manual, and there is a lot more to safe boating than that.

There are great free launch areas on Emerald Isle and at Cedar Point. The favorite boats in the area are flat-bottomed skiffs like my boat or bay boats with a slight V hull. I have a skiff with a little V in the bow to improve control and the ride in rough water.

Boats like mine draw very little water or in non-boater language, they will run safely in very shallow water.

It is a very good thing to have a boat that draws less than two feet of water because there are plenty of places here where water less than two feet can sneak up on you. It is also very handy to have a GPS with a depth finder that really works. If you boat here a lot, it is not if you are going to get caught on a sandbar but when one will snag you. I got caught in the summer of 2012 when the sun blinded me while making a turn. I was happy that I had a Sea Tow membership and by using their smartphone app, their captain found me without any difficulty. Still it was a beautiful place to be stuck. My oldest daughter whom you can see in the photo below by squinting had a ball walking around on the shallow water islands.

In the fall of 2013, I switched my towing service to BoatsU.S. They actually keep a towboat in the Swansboro area and it is usually parked at Casper's Marina. They are very familiar with our local waters. Their phone number is (252) 728-5088 but if you are planning boating in the area, it is a lot less expensive to get a membership instead of calling them after you are stuck.

We have some very nicely marked channels. It is easy to hop on the Intracoastal Waterway and head east for a nice trip to Shackleford Banks, which is one of the true jewels of the Crystal Coast. That trip takes you through the Morehead City Harbor and depending on your boat can last between 1.5 and 2 hours if you are leaving from Swansboro harbor. It is even possible to go down to Wilmington for lunch.

However, there are some much less ambitious trips that are fun. If you don't have a GPS with area maps, pick up a map of Bogue Inlet so you will have a general idea of the area. Assuming you have a sea worthy boat of sixteen feet or longer and the proper safety gear, launch at Cedar Point Wildlife Resources Ramp and head left towards the Emerald Isle Bridge. In just under nine tenths of a mile you will see a large marked channel on your starboard side. Guide your boat into that channel which takes you out to the Point area. Don't get confused by the marked entrance to the Coast Guard Channel. It splits off to the east or portside not long after you have started the journey.

If you follow the Bogue Inlet channel just over 1.8 miles with the marsh on your starboard side and a series of sandbars on your port side, you will eventually cut back to the south towards the ocean. Not long after you cut south, you will see a long strand of sand on your starboard side. If you are careful, it is very easy to work your boat up to that strand of sand.

The standard procedure is to nose your boat up to the sand, unload the anchor and everyone jump off but the captain.

Back your boat off the sand so it floats, tilt your motor, and have someone secure the anchor a safe distance inland. Then use the anchor line to pull the boat to shore so the captain can jump off the boat. You still need to know whether the tide is coming in or going out.

You will see lots of folks who completely beach their boats. You see some of the same people struggling to launch their beached boat if they have not paid enough attention to the tides. Be mindful that it you try to anchor near the main channel for Bogue Inlet that there is a lot of current there. The water there in places can be thirty feet deep so make sure you have the proper amount of line to have the anchor safely set. You can have a look at some of the maps of our boating trips in our Kindle version. Use my maps only for general guidance. The channels are always moving down here so watch for shallow water and take your time. We found that out this spring when we cut over from the Point area to the main channel behind Bear Island. The sandbar that I got stuck on three years ago has grown farther eastward.

It would be a rare day in the busy part of summer when at least one or two boats were not anchored in that area of Bear Island near the Inlet. Sometimes there are a lot of boats there on weekends like the Fourth of July. A trip out to the Point-Bogue Inlet area will actually give you lots of ideas about where you can anchor and enjoy the beach. There are plenty of good spots. Sometimes we anchor on a sandbar that is barely above water. The water is warm and some folks even put a beach chair in the shallow water.

One word of caution, it is possible to get from the spot you turned south near the Point to the unbelievably scenic area behind Hammock Beach-Bear Island. However, the safest way is to follow a local boater who is headed there with his boat up on plane. There are some shallow spots and even if you know where you are going, you can get pretty stuck like I did a few summers ago. If you get stuck, it is nice to have a BoatsU.S. or a Sea Tow membership. Waiting for the tide to come and rescue you can take hours and not having a membership with one of the towing companies can cost you hundreds of dollars.

Another really nice and easy boat ride is to take your boat west 2.65 miles down the Intracoastal Waterway from Swansboro Harbor to the very well-marked Cow Channel, which takes you to Bear Island. It is pretty easy boating, and you can see some of the most beautiful water in the area. It is a much easier way for a first trip to the back of Bear Island than coming from the Point area. Cow Channel is marked on one of my online maps linked to from our Kindle version. Again please heed my warning to use this only as general guidance. We tried this route in the spring of 2016 and had no problems, but things change fast around here. On our way back to Swansboro we saw an osprey that was so big from a distance that we thought he was an eagle.

With all the boating that is available out in the marshes, few boaters except locals go up the White Oak River. However, the channel is well marked, and there is a deep hole near the red sixteen buoy that is locally known as the croaker hole.

Before you go boating, know that chances on the weekend or holidays are good that the Coast Guard and/or the Wildlife Resources people will stop your boat for a safety check. Make certain that you check your safety equipment including the date on your flares. Your throw pillow needs to be in good shape and not stowed. Youngsters are required to be wearing life jackets. You will always see me wearing my red life suspenders. I try to never leave the dock without a full complement of safety equipment. If you are going to be boating near dusk, make sure that your navigation lights work including the bow running lights and do not forget a working flashlight.

Headed out Bogue Inlet.

Feeding the Fish, Otherwise Known as Fishing

With all the beach and water in Carteret County, it is no surprise that people like to try fishing when visiting the area. It is fun, easy, and often keeps dad busy while the ladies and children enjoy the beach or even visit the local shops.

Before I give you my advice that is slanted towards my home turf, the White Oak River, I am pleased to offer this opening from one of Emerald Isle's true experts, Dr. Bogus. He fishes almost every day of the year.

"Of the alluring beach activities in summery Emerald Isle, fishing or actually catching fish may top the list after sunning on the beautiful sandy beaches and possibly surfing. Summertime has a potpourri of fish from bottom feeders like the tasty and feisty sea mullet pompano, spots and black drum to more predatory fish like marauding schools of Spanish mackerel and bluefish, as well as our state fish, red drum and ambushing foraging flounder."

"Baits can either accommodate the preference of the fish or the adventuresome nature of the angler. For the leisurely, most use the universal bait; cut pieces of shrimp on a standard two-hook bottom rig with a 3-ounce pyramid sinker. There isn't anything out there worth catching that won't eat shrimp. For the more adventurous, hunting down mole crabs along the surf will be fun, especially for the kids and ensure catches of sea mullet both drums and pompano. For those like me that want more hands-on action, there is a tackle box full of artificial baits including MirrOlures, soft plastics on a lead head jig and a very popular heavy metal favorite, the Kastmaster. Tackle is simple, just a 7- or 8-foot medium action rod with 10- or 12-pound test and a 4000-size reel will handle most expected catches."

"Where? Emerald Isle has several prime locations for catching. First is the Pointe area at the very west end of Coast Guard Rd. along Bogue Inlet. Next are the two public, eastern and western ocean access areas with facilities and plenty of parking, and don't forget Bogue Inlet Fishing Pier. Bogue Pier, which has been a popular fishing location for over 50-years and provides access to all the above species depending where you choose to fish and a real plus offers the opportunity to tackle big game fish like 20- or 30-pound king mackerel, tarpon, cobia and other big fish out at the very far end of the pier, 'kingland'."

"If you have questions or need expert lessons to make your summer fishing experience a memorable, give longtime local pier, surf and kayak fishing expert Dr. Bogus a call (252.354.4905)."

As Dr. Bogus indicates we have as many types of fishing as we have kinds of water. You can fish in the surf, the ocean, the sound, the rivers, or the marshes. Some types of fishing require a boat, but many others do not.

First off, you do need a saltwater fishing license unless you are fishing off a licensed pier like the Bogue Inlet Fishing Pier or on a boat that covers it. An annual saltwater license is ten dollars for state residents. Non-residents can get a ten-day license for ten dollars. The same ten-day license is five dollars for state residents. If you are sixty-five or over, the license you buy lasts you for as long as you can fish.

Dudley's Marina in Swansboro or Reel Outdoors in Emerald Isle can help with licenses, gear and information. You can buy a very usable fishing rod and reel for thirty to forty dollars, but it will not last forever.

If you want serious fishing advice on tackle and care about what is biting, Reel Outdoors is the best place to visit. Usually the people behind the counter are fisherman. I buy my gear there because they stand behind what they sell. You can get inexpensive gear there, but you also can get very good gear that will last for years. The Penn spinning reel that I got there is my go to reel and I have had it for a few years. They have a wide selection. They also know what is happening in area waters. Just to make things easier they have a nice shop to distract the ladies and the Village Market, a very good place to eat breakfast or lunch.

Beyond a rod and reel, you need a little terminal tackle. The easiest thing is to buy a couple of double hook bottom rigs. Get a pack of hooks and two or three weights. You will need at least two or three pyramid shaped weights. If you are only getting two, go for one each of three and four ounces. If you are getting three weights, add one two-ounce weight for times when there is less current. A bucket and a sand spike for your rod will complete your gear.

If you want to get fancy, you can either add a second rod and attach a Gotcha plug for bluefish or add a heavy-duty snap to the line on your rod so you can switch to an artificial lure quickly if you see some bluefish cruising the beach.

Next you need some bait. This is where I might diverge from the standard advice which would to be go buy some bait shrimp or frozen squid. I always buy top quality food grade shrimp for my bait. I usually like to buy a pound and one half and have the heads removed. Then I take a little less than half of the shrimp and pack it in ice for the beach. The rest I pack in a cooler that I leave at home. I take very good care of my bait shrimp and at the end of the day if I haven't caught any fish, I will still have some nice shrimp to eat. As the local wisdom says if you won't eat it, the fish likely won't either.

Next head out to the beach, park yourself close to the water and look for a nice slough of water running parallel with the shore between the beach and an off beach sandbar. If you can find a cut in one of those bars, that is also helpful. The cut will usually be a productive spot. You do not have to be able to cast a mile to fish. Most of the fish are between that first bar and the shore.

The best advice on tides and fishing is to fish when the water is moving, either coming in or going out. Fish also respond to bait. If there is no bait in the area, fishing might be slow. Bird feeding on the water are a good sign of bait.

However, if you throw a rig baited with a couple of small pieces of shrimp in the surf along the beaches at Emerald Isle, you will likely catch something. If you are lucky you might catch a keeper flounder like the one pictured below or a red drum. More likely you will catch a pompano, spot, or bluefish depending on the time of the year.

You can also vary your bait by using sand fleas that you can capture in the surf or even artificial bloodworms that you buy in packages.

Here are a few other tips that might make your fishing experience more enjoyable. If a four-ounce weight will not hold your rig on the bottom, you might be better off waiting for a day with less current, wind, or surf. If you keep missing small bites, you might want to switch to a smaller hook or something less attractive to pinfish like a white plastic Gulp. Do not be afraid to ask other anglers or the stores what is biting and what bait is working best. What you hear will be invaluable information and most people are happy to share it. Fishing advice is like gold when it come from experts.

There are plenty of other ways to fish in the area. You can fish by kayak, from the Bogue Inlet Pier, take a morning ride on the Nancy Lee party boat or hire one of the many competent area guides. I have enjoyed a couple of amazing fishing trips with Captain Tom Roller of Waterdog Guide Service in Beaufort. There are plenty of guides with boats around the Swansboro area, just ask in the marinas or at Reel Outdoors.

Remember you can even hire our local surf expert, Dr. Bogus. He will provide some real surf fishing training. He also is often involved in fishing seminars and probably knows how to read a beach better than anyone that I know.

If you have a skiff, there are plenty of options from drift fishing for flounder in the Inlet to trolling for Spanish mackerel just off the beaches. If you can purchase or find some mud minnows, they are often deadly on flounders during the summer.

Fishing from the Bogue Inlet Pier is another option and an experience in itself. A new neighbor of mine landed over forty bluefish one day on the pier in the spring of 2016. A daily fishing pass is $10. No license is required with the pass. The pass allows you to use two rods and includes children under six for free. You can even rent a rod and reel. Walking onto the pier is free and is a good way to figure out what is being caught. It is also a great way to decide whether or not you want to go pier fishing or surf fishing.

If you love kayaks and fishing, our area is a perfect place to take advantage of your skills. There is plenty marsh to fish around here, but I have been most successful fishing the oyster rocks in the White Oak River. I caught several drum and trout there over the years including this very nice cooler full one evening.

Usually around the middle to the end of May I will catch my my first fish of this season from the White Oak. Last year it was a flounder and a couple of years ago it was a very nice 21″ Red Drum.

When I caught the drum I was fishing a small cut between two oyster rocks in the White Oak. There was strong current flowing down river through the cut. My second cast was down river and I retrieved against the current. The drum hit hard like they usually do. That was all it took and the battle was on. The drum did run the wrong way and got on the other side of the oyster rock from me. After a number of long runs, I paddled the kayak with one arm to the other end of the oyster rock and worked him around to my side where I could slide the net under him after a few more enthusiastic runs. It was a well-fought battle that I will long remember. It will be great fodder for fish stories for many years.

My drum was caught on a jig head with a white pogy gulp. I lost a few squiggly tails off swimming mullet gulps earlier to nuisance fish and switched to the pogy gulp just before catching the drum. In the fall of 2014 in the same spot, one evening I caught 19" and 21" trout and a 20" drum (cooler picture). They were all caught on Tsunami plastic. It is easy to see why I am a fan of the river.

2014 was a great season drum and I caught my second drum of the year within a few days of the first. That drum was 22" and was caught on Tsunami soft plastic swim bait. The next year, 2015, was a tougher fishing year. We had over seven feet of rain and it kept the salinity level of the river down too low for really good fishing. I caught some drum but did not bring home a keeper drum. I did get catch some nice flounder. This year has started slow but I took my neighbor out fishing in the middle of May and he caught a 17" trout which he let me have for dinner along with a bluefish for appetizer fish bites

No matter what kind of fishing you choose, you'll likely have fun. If you don't catch anything, either eat the shrimp or go visit Jimmy at Clyde Phillips Seafood. A flounder from Jimmy is almost as good as one you catch yourself. Some summers they have gigged flounder which I like better than gill netted flounder. It is certainly a more sustainable fishery.

If you have rented a home with a dock and want to do some crabbing just for fun, crab traps are pretty inexpensive and you will find turkey necks or something similar at Piggly-Wiggly. You likely will not catch enough to eat but you will gain some respect of crab claws when you release them from the trap.

My Favorite Day Trip and a Few Others

If you need more stimulation than a beach, there are a number of wonderful places to visit. Many of my favorites are within easy driving distance.

The one place that we almost always take visitors is Beaufort. While it is only eighteen miles away, it does take thirty-five to forty minutes to get there because you have to drive through Morehead City and over the Gallant's Channel Drawbridge which often catches travelers. They are making great progress on a new bridge but it will be a while before we can enjoy it.

Morehead City is serious about their speed limits so be mindful of that when traveling through the city. It is a good idea to keep a watchful eye on your speedometer in most of our area. Highway 24 between Cape Carteret and Morehead City is well patrolled by the NC Highway Patrol, and you will not be on Emerald Isle long before you figure out that the Emerald Isle police are very serious about keeping residents and tourists safe from speeders.

There are two ways to get to Beaufort from the Cape Carteret-Emerald Isle area. The first route would be to go east along Highway 58 (Emerald Drive) which parallels the beaches through Salter Path, Pine Knoll Shores, and cross the bridge at Atlantic Beach to Morehead City and turn right onto Highway 70 which takes you across the bridges into Beaufort. That route can sometimes seem like it takes forever even if you start halfway down the beach. The other route is

Highway 24 East that runs into Highway 70 East on the outskirts of Morehead City. Your route choice depends on where you are and what you want to do besides go to Beaufort. We often go one way and come back the other at least during the winter. Summertime we usually stick to Highway 24. They are building a new bridge to Beaufort and the construction has the causeway down to two lanes so expect slow traffic.

Obviously for a few years you will still have to cross the old drawbridge just before you get to Beaufort. Once you get across, you will find a busy little town on the water as you can see from the next picture that was taken from the nearby Duke Marine Lab. After crossing the drawbridge, take the first right off of Highway 70 and keep driving slowly until you have no choice but to turn left or right. You'll be on Front Street, Beaufort's main street. If you turn left and drive along the wide avenue, the water will be on your right and several stately homes will be on your left.

When you first turn left on Front Street there are usually some parking spots. Beaufort has gone to parking meters. I have not tried enough spots to know if they are everywhere, but there are plenty of them and parking is going to be a dollar an hour. Finding a parking spot can be a challenge in Beaufort depending on the day, the weather, and what is scheduled. There are two small lots closer to the center of town. They definitely have meters and will be active starting Memorial Day weekend 2016. Those lots are right on the waterfront adjacent to the boardwalk. Beyond that there is street parking that extends well beyond the core of the downtown. There is another large lot a few blocks off the street on Turner Street. However, sometimes the church and town are feuding and it can be unavailable.

My suggestion is to cruise down Front Street until you pass the Inlet Inn and the very tasteful BB&T Bank. Take a left on Pollock Street just after the bank then the next left on Ann St. Stay on Ann Street for four or five blocks and take another left which will bring you back to Front St. Then pick a parking place that suits your needs after you have scoped out the town a little.

There is plenty to do in Beaufort, and one of the great things is that you can park your car and walk to it all assuming it is not a really hot atypical Crystal Coast day.

One of my favorite things on either a very hot or rainy day is to visit the Maritime Museum that is located on Front Street between Turner and Orange Street. If you are headed there, there is some parking at the museum. The museum is a wonderful free lesson in the maritime history of the area.

Even my son who is in his thirties loves the Maritime Museum.

Just across the street from the museum is the boat-building annex. There is usually something interesting going on there, but there is a fee to go inside. If by the time you finish at the museum, you are hungry for lunch or dinner, there are a number of tasty options available.

However, you should know before you dine that Beaufort is not known for inexpensive dining options. If you look across Front Street from the Maritime Museum, you will see the Front Street Grill at Stillwater and a little beyond it to the right is the Spouter Inn. Both are excellent choices to dine on the water. The Spouter Inn is probably my favorite of the two, but the atmosphere of Front Street is very nice. We have some nice memories from eating on the deck at the Spouter Inn at sunset on a few warm summer evenings.

Other options that we can recommend are Beaufort Grocery, a block or so off Front Street on Queen Street. We have had some nice lunches at Clawson's 1905 Restaurant and Pub which is on Front Street before you get to Queen Street has good food, but probably not as exceptional as the first three restaurants. Though it has been years since we have eaten there, we enjoyed a couple of great meals at Blue Moon Bistro. On our list to try in Beaufort is the Old Salt Restaurant and Oyster Bar.

The only inexpensive place to eat with character that I would recommend is No Name Pizza and Subs. You have to get back in your car and drive back out to Highway 70, and it is on your right after Highway 70 takes a sharp right on its way east. There is also a No Name in Morehead City.

Tucked along Front Street you will find numerous interesting shops. My wife enjoys wandering through the shops which change a little each time we write the guide. I like, Scuttlebut, which has "nautical books and bounty." We both usually visit the Beaufort Trading Company and take a walk down the boardwalk to see all the fancy boats docked there. Sometimes we buy some fudge from the Fudge Factory by the water or get an ice cream cone at the little shop just off the boardwalk. It is the only shop that I have seen sell ice cream by weight.

The Beaufort Historic Site and their gift shop are always a treat. The Beaufort Historical Association also runs a double-decker London tour bus that provides tours of the town. Walking through the old Burial Grounds is also fun. One of my favorite things to do is a water tour of the Beaufort area. You can get a neat boat ride at Waterbug Tours.

With the consolidation of ferry services done by the National Park Service a few years ago, the Waterbug is now on the eastern end of town at 610 Front Street across from the Inlet Inn. You can still easily catch a ferry to Cape Lookout or one of the closer places like Shackleford Banks. Island Express Ferry won the National Park service contract so they now are the only ferry traveling from Beaufort to Cape Lookout. They also provide service from Harkers Island.

Once you decide to leave Beaufort, continue on Front Street in the opposite direction from where you first entered town. It is a nice leisurely ride along Taylor's Creek and the stately homes. Eventually Front Street curves back to the left of the boat ramp. It runs into Lennoxville Road. Take a left there and follow Lennoxville Road until it runs into Highway 70 at a stoplight in about 1.5 miles. Take a left on Highway 70 at the stoplight and follow it back to Morehead City. While driving along Front Street towards Lennoxville Road, it is not unusual to see some of the wild horses. The picture below was taken in the spring of 2014.

Also if you decide to spend the night in Beaufort, we can highly recommend the Beaufort Inn.

If you are coming back from Beaufort, just before Highway 24 takes a left off of Highway 70, there is a Harris-Teeter Grocery store on your right. We enjoy shopping at HT once in a while just for variety. They have very good produce. If you have remembered your cooler with ice, grocery shopping on your day trip is an option.

If you want some of your typical mall stores, such as Best Buy, Belks, TJ Maxx, Wal-Mart, and Bed, Bath, and Beyond, you will find them in the area along both Highways 24 and

70. Most of the stores are in the "V" formed by the intersection of the two highways, but there are growing numbers on the north side of Highway 70 west after Highway 24 splits off.

There is no shortage of restaurants. You will find an Olive Garden, Ruby Tuesday's, Panera Bread, Buffalo Wild Wings, Five Guys, Starbucks, Chick-fil-A, Applebee's, and Panera among others.

If you get on Highway 70, miss the Highway 24 turnoff, and want to get back to Highway 24, you can turn at the stoplight that takes you to Lowe's Home Improvement. If you miss that and are still on Highway 70 west of the shopping centers, watch for Lookout Ford on your left and turn left onto McCabe Road. It will take you back to Highway 24. Once you get to Highway 24 make a right turn to head back to Emerald by way of Highway 24. It is less than fourteen miles from McCabe Road to the stoplight where you turn to get on the Emerald Isle Bridge. The total distance from where Highway 24 splits off from Highway 70 is a little less than seventeen miles.

While Beaufort is one of my favorite trips, there are some others that are well worth considering if you are here on the coast long enough to have wanderlust strike.

One easy trip that my wife and I have enjoyed is driving up to Harkers Island and taking a small skiff ferry for the short ride over to Cape Lookout. We have not been over since the National Park Service consolidated ferry services. Island

Express Ferry is providing ferry service from Harkers Island to Cape Lookout. I know Cape Lookout will not change in response to different ferry service.

One surprising day trip that is not that overly difficult is one that takes you to Nags Head. The drive is just a little over three hours. My wife and I have driven over to have lunch with friends, walked Jeanette's Pier and viewed a few favorite spots and made it home in plenty of time to relax before bed.

We also enjoy going to Tryon Palace, but we do prefer going early in the spring before the weather gets hot. Tryon Palace is a little over an hour of driving from Emerald Isle. I prefer the route which takes you up Route 58 and in on Route 17 purely because it takes me by my favorite local bagel shop, The Carolina Bagel Shop. Moore's Barbecue, a good wood-fired barbecue spot, is in the midst of new construction, but are planning to re-open by July 2016.

Another great historical trip is visiting Edenton. The trip following Google map directions is less than 2.5 hours. The waterfront and Cupola House gardens early in the year are well worth the trip. The next picture is the waterfront in Edenton. We have managed to combine a trip to Ocracoke by the ferry, then Nags Head and a visit to historic Edenton on the way home.

Another of my favorite spots is Ocracoke Island, but it is really an overnight trip. There is a ferry from Cedar Island to Ocracoke and then there are plenty of almost empty beaches to wander. Ocracoke has added services in recent years but the town is still the same size. The result is that there is a lot crammed into a very small village. The streets are a strange mix of golf carts, bikes, walkers, cars, buses, delivery trucks, and trucks hauling boats. Ocracoke is still a tiny spot way out in the ocean with not a lot of restaurants and only a couple of places to buy groceries. We did visit Ocracoke in early summer of 2013. We stayed in the Pony Island Motel that happened to be the only place on the island with a TV in July of 1969. I came down from the Ocracoke campground and checked in for a night so I could see Neil Armstrong step on the moon. It was not the greatest viewing experience given the poor TV reception on Ocracoke in those days but I got to see a historic moment and it is a great memory.

Even More Shopping & Entertainment

Shopping is not a high priority in my life so it has ended up towards the end of my guide. I mentioned the shopping in the Morehead City area, but most people do not come to the beach to shop Best Buy or TJ Maxx. The ladies of our family like to wander the unique area shops and browse for hours on end.

Fortunately, in the Emerald Isle area there are options besides going to the nice shops in Beaufort. There are plenty of equally cute shops in Swansboro, Emerald Isle, and Cedar Point.

I am not going to attempt a comprehensive list, but I suggest lunch at the Ice House or the attached Boro on Front Street in Swansboro. After your meal, take a leisurely stroll along the main street. While there are only a handful of shops, there seems to be plenty to keep my wife and our guests busy. One different shop that the men might enjoy is Poor Man's Hole. It has many unique old collectables.

Moving down the street, there are lots of shops from Russell's Olde Tyme Shoppe to The Mercantile, Bake, Bottle, & Brew, and The Salty Sheep Yarn Shop around the corner on Church Street. Church Street also has a Beaufort Olive Oil store and the Church Street Deli, Irish Pub & Inn. There is even a cigar shop on Church Street. Just start walking and browsing. There is even a new candy specialty shop, Candy Edventure.

If you want a little excitement, you can walk out on the town pier, or for even more excitement follow the sidewalk under the Highway 24 Bridge to Centennial Park. Unfortunately, the fishing pier had to be torn down for safety reasons. Down by Saltwater Grill, you might find a couple of sailboats or a cruiser tied up at the new town dock which seems to finally be getting some visitors. You will often find some evening music in Swansboro even when there is no concert scheduled by the town.

There are lots of restaurant choices for lunch in Swansboro including The Boro, Icehouse, Yana's, Saltwater Grill, Church Street Deli, and Swansboro Food & Beverage Co.

If you want to venture out by car, there are a number of interesting places especially in Cedar Point on your way back to Emerald Isle from Swansboro. Jeff and Mary who used to run Salty Aire Market have moved up the road and now run

The Market at 1046 Cedar Point Blvd which is a lot closer to the island. You will find some great food trucks around their location at times. They have local produce and grass fed meat, organic eggs, and other goodies. Nice weekends you can expect to find several vendors there.

You will several more shops in Cedar Point. Christina's is now Christina's Wine Boutique. If you are trying to keep dad happy, stop at Harrika's Brew House. It was recently rated one of the top 100 beer bars in the United States. One of the unique brews from there might wash away all his memories of shopping.

We sometimes stop at the Coastal Outlet at Cedar Point.

It is on the left just after you pass Walston's Hardware on the right. You will recognize either by its pink color or by the red trolley bus parked in front. Amazing things are hiding in that pink building.

I snapped this next picture of the Emerald Plantation directory on an April 17, 2016 visit. It is as close as I can come to a real time update of what is in Emerald Plantation.

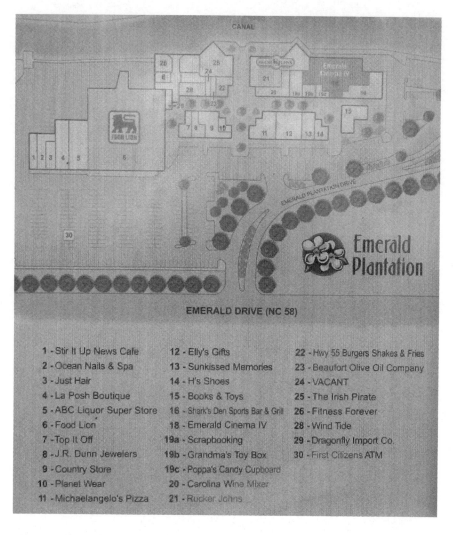

1 - Stir It Up News Cafe
2 - Ocean Nails & Spa
3 - Just Hair
4 - La Posh Boutique
5 - ABC Liquor Super Store
6 - Food Lion
7 - Top It Off
8 - J.R. Dunn Jewelers
9 - Country Store
10 - Planet Wear
11 - Michaelangelo's Pizza

12 - Elly's Gifts
13 - Sunkissed Memories
14 - H's Shoes
15 - Books & Toys
16 - Shark's Den Sports Bar & Grill
18 - Emerald Cinema IV
19a - Scrapbooking
19b - Grandma's Toy Box
19c - Poppa's Candy Cupboard
20 - Carolina Wine Mixer
21 - Rucker Johns

22 - Hwy 55 Burgers Shakes & Fries
23 - Beaufort Olive Oil Company
24 - VACANT
25 - The Irish Pirate
26 - Fitness Forever
28 - Wind Tide
29 - Dragonfly Import Co.
30 - First Citizens ATM

Highway 55 Burgers in Emerald Plantation is a good spot and if Ryan, the owner, is cooking, the burgers are the top of my best buy in burgers list.

Everything you might need is in Emerald Plantation aside from fishing tackle (you will find the best fishing gear at Reel Outdoors down the street), electronics (Best Buy or Staples in Morehead City), hardware goods (there is a great Ace Hardware just on the right as you turn into Emerald Plantation at the light), bedding (Coastal Outlet in Cedar Point), and auto accessories (take your pick of auto stores in Cedar Point, Swansboro, and Cape Carteret). There is even one of those rare things, an independent book store, Emerald Isle Books and Toys located right in Emerald Plantation. They are also well stocked with toys and puzzles. They are close to Shark's Den (think wings) and the movie theater.

And after a hard day of shopping, I might suggest an ice cream cone at either Ben and Jerry's or Sweet Spot. They are located across Emerald Drive from from each other just before the turn to the Bogue Inlet Pier. You can do double duty at Sweet Spot. While dad and the kids have an ice cream cone, mom and any other ladies can shop the gifts. Personally I like their fresh taffy collection better, but the ladies in the family would disagree with me. There is a Dairy Queen on the right just before Sweet Spot if you are driving up the beach. If all of these ice cream spots are crowded, turn around, drive a little and visit the best value for ice cream in the area, Waters Ace Hardware, in Swansboro. I checked current prices just before Memorial Day. A single scoop is still only $1.25. They only have eight flavors but even two scoops are only $1.75. I am fond of their banana pudding flavor. While there check out their Sourwood honey and North Carolina peanuts. They close at 5:30 PM weekdays and at 5:00 PM on Saturdays. They are not open on Sundays.

There are two eighteen-hole golf courses nearby. Dad and the guys might enjoy a round of golf instead of shopping. Silver Creek Golf Club is at 601 Peletier Loop Road about four miles north on Highway 58 from the intersection with Highway 24. Their phone number is 252 393- 8058. They welcome visiting golfers. The course is close to my house, and I have never seen it crowded. Star Hill Golf Course is located just off Taylor Notion Road, which is a shortcut between Highway 58 and Highway 24 headed to Morehead City. Go north up Highway 58 about 1.25 miles turn right on Taylor Notion and watch for signs to the club. They also welcome visitors, and their phone number is 252 393-8111.

Of course there are go-carts and miniature golf courses located all around the area, but I haven't tried any of them. The big water slide on Emerald Isle might not be open this summer due to some safety issues, but I have never figured out their schedule anyway. If the weather is very hot, they are usually open but the biggest slide will not be until repaired. Going for a walk on the Bogue Inlet Pier is also a good way to break up the day. It is free unless you want to fish. The last picture on Page 122 is looking east from the pier and was taken at Thanksgiving 2015.

Oh No, It's Raining at the Beach

Sometimes rain happens even in our paradise. While we work hard to schedule all precipitation events at night, sometimes things don't turn out as planned.

There are some options. One of the easiest things to do is take the kids to MacDaddy's in Cape Carteret for bowling and games. It is very clean and well run, and they even have some good food.

One of the favorite options in the rain is to head to the North Carolina Aquarium in Pine Knoll Shores. The drive is a little over fourteen miles from the stop light at Coast Guard Road in Emerald Isle. The Aquarium is a wonderful place to visit, and even when it is crowded, it is possible to enjoy the exhibits. When the Aquarium is crowded, we have had some luck going later in the day around 3 PM but that only gives you a couple of hours to see everything. However, two hours in the Aquarium might be enough depending on the attention span of your children.

You can combine a visit to Fort Macon with a visit to the Aquarium, but much of the neatest parts of the fort are outside. There are some very nice things to see in parts of the fort that will keep you dry, but you might get wet getting to them. Fort Macon is worth a trip during good weather. There is also a great beach access there and good fishing along the shore.

You can wander the shops at Emerald Plantation in the rain, grab lunch at Highway 55 Burgers or a nice salad Rucker John's and catch a movie there.

There is a Carmike Cinema 6 about twenty-two miles away in Havelock. The drive will take a little less than thirty minutes. It is a newer theater with more movies. It is also next door to a very nice Smithfield's Barbecue and Chicken. Smithfield's has very good Eastern North Carolina style barbecue. They also fry some tasty chicken. A trip to the movies and dinner at Smithfield's is not a bad choice if you do not want to go to MacDaddy's or the Aquarium.

Jacksonville also has theaters and lots of restaurants and the traffic to match. You can combine a trip to Target, Sam's Club, Home Depot, or Barnes and Noble with a trip to the mall or lunch but that is probably a lot like being at home. We enjoy Marakesh for an interesting lunch, Jimmy Johns for a quick sub, Firehouse Subs for hot subs, and Jesses for a gyro. Jacksonville traffic can be notoriously bad. If you cannot live without a Target, there is a back way which avoids almost all of the Western Boulevard traffic. The new bypass and connector have helped but Western Boulevard still can move slowly.

Another option is to visit the Western Carteret Library on Taylor Notion Road. Besides books, they have computers, WIFI, and sometimes activities for children. There are no fees for visitors to use the library and you just need proper identification to get a library card. They are open 8:30 AM to 5:00 PM Monday, Wednesday, Friday, and Saturday. On Tuesday and Thursday, they are open until 8:00 PM. Their phone number is 252 393- 6500.

As you can see, there is plenty to do in the area even when it rains. Most of our rains are not daylong downpours. Occasionally we even have rain that does not come in the night as we all hope it does. Still as long as there is no thunder or lightning, a walk in the light, warm rain on the beach is not a bad fate.

Weather at the Beach

We generally have very nice weather along the Crystal Coast. It is rare that the temperatures get much above ninety along the beaches. Still it is very hard to generalize about the weather on the coast. The best time I have found to be out boating and fishing is early in the morning or late in the evening.

It is not unusual to have afternoon thunderstorms, which start around 3 PM. That is our normal summer pattern. That means that enjoying the early part of the day gives you the best odds of having really good weather. We often have a 30-40% chance of thunderstorms in the afternoon. Depending on what front is moving through the area, we can have a morning or even nighttime thunderstorms.

North Carolina thunderstorms can be impressive especially at night. We had some wild ones over the years so be prepared. I was recently caught out on the White Oak River in a rainstorm. It was a long wet paddle to my dock. I was lucky no thunder or lightning was involved. If you are on the water or on the beach and see a line of thunderstorms coming, get off the water and off the beach. I use a great little app on my Android Smartphone. It's called Radar Now, and I can quickly get a look at the weather in the area. Just keep an eye on the horizon and don't gamble on being able to outrun storms. Not every evening on the White Oak is like the following picture.

If you are going to be boating, pay attention to the winds and tides. I will not take my skiff out when the winds are over 15 miles per hour unless there is a really good reason. It is no fun being caught on the water in bad weather and it is dangerous. Being out at a low tide also requires a little more diligence.

We don't have a lot of fog here on the Crystal Coast. When we do get fogged in, it usually burns off by mid-morning.

Our weather rarely gets stuck in a rut, but we do have a lot of blue-sky days with a 30% chance of thunderstorms. For a couple of dry years, even the chance of summer thunderstorms was pretty slim. In 2011 we went from May 7 to June 19 with just one quarter of an inch of rain. The spring of 2012 we enjoyed exceptional weather at the beginning and at the end. The summer of 2012 was a more normal summer with enough precipitation to please those of us who garden and have to worry about yards growing in the sand. As hard as it is to believe we almost washed away on the mainland with over 92 inches of rain in 2015. Emerald Isle fared slightly better but it was still wet year in this area. This year, 2016, started out with normal precipitation but it turned cool in May and we saw few truly warm days until early June. I have not even gotten a ripe tomato and it is June 4. Even Bonnie, the tropical depression/storm, gave us mostly sunshine for Memorial Day weekend. Parts of Emerald Isle got very little rain. Along the White Oak River on the mainland Bonnie provided a modest 2.2 inches over three days. Most of it came on Wednesday, June 1, after Memorial Day. Hatteras got over ten inches from the same storm. It all depends on the track and where the swirl of precipitation ends up.

The one thing most people worry about the most when coming to the beach is a hurricane. By fall we will have been here ten years. A couple of storms have swung close enough to the beach to cause mandatory evacuations of Emerald Isle. In August 2011, we rode out Hurricane Irene. In the fall of 2012, Hurricane Sandy brushed the area. Irene was a very impressive storm, but as I like to tell my inland friends, we have very big drains down here on the coast. The White Oak River at nearly two miles wide where we live is just one of the drains. In addition to the big drains, we have a good system of barrier islands covered with lots of vegetation.

While I have seen flooding on Coast Guard Road on Emerald Isle, Emerald Isle keeps improving their pumping ability for low areas and the flooding on Emerald Isle pales to the flooding that I have seen in our former mountain home of Roanoke, Virginia. Emerald Isle continues to do what is necessary to keep visitors and residents safe during storms.

In general flooding is more of a problem as you move inland from the coast. Where narrow rivers collect vast amounts of rain and there is no tide to take it out, you can have serious flooding. On the coast we worry more about wind than rain. Our subdivision endured a freak storm six years ago. We got over twenty inches of rain in less than eight hours. While it was a lot of water, we did not have serious flooding. If the peak of the rain had been earlier before the tide started going out or if the winds had been blowing the sound into the river, it might have been different.

The Neuse River, which flows by New Bern, does have some challenges when the winds try to push all the water from Pamlico Sound into it. Fortunately, geography helps prevent a situation like that for us. We don't have a huge body of water with a direct shot at the White Oak River.

On the coast there will always be the chance of a hurricane. The good news with hurricanes when compared to tornadoes is that we have substantial warning when a hurricane is headed our way. If you are renting a vacation home and there is a mandatory evacuation, you have no choice but to leave. It is for everyone's safety.

In high winds they will close the Emerald Isle Bridge so if you are told to leave, just be safe and leave. Likely you will be able to quickly return. The area got through Hurricane Irene in good shape compared to many places, but you never know what will happen with the next storm.

One final note on the weather is well worth emphasizing. If you have the flexibility to vacation in the fall, it is one of the great times to visit the beach. Any crowds disappear after Labor Day and are replaced by fishermen that do not come close to matching the numbers of vacationers. The ocean waters are usually warm all through October and well into November most years. Sometimes the air temperature is very pleasant on into December. Many of us think fall is the best season at the beach.

It is hard to beat a warm, sunny, fall day on the beach when there is no humidity in the air, and the sky is the bright blue color typical of a fall day. Of course there is the added benefit that if you like to fish, the fishing is almost always much better in the fall. Many of us live for fall trout fishing. All our fish, including flounder, grow a lot by the fall and seem to be much easier to catch.

Emergency Information & Miscellaneous Notes

It is impossible to include everything about an area in a travel guide. There are also things that just don't fit neatly in any section. This section is where I have stuck everything for which I can't find another place.

Last year there were a couple of decks that collapsed at rental houses on Emerald Isle. The Town and owners have worked very hard this year to make certain the issue with decks on rental homes was resolved before the vacation season.

While I do not have a special section on accessibility, there is accessible parking at many of the public beach access points. The Town of Emerald Isle has a list of all the accesses on their website. Both the Eastern and Western Regional access have ramps they make it easier to get on the beach. The Town of Emerald Isle has free loaner beach wheel chairs available on a first come, first served basis at the Fire Department. Their phone number is 252-354-2445. Certainly the whole Emerald Woods trail is accessible as is the bike trail and the Bogue Inlet Pier.

When it comes to medical issues, there are a number of doctors and walk in clinics in the area. We only have experience with one. My wife and I go to Cape Carteret Family Medicine, 1057 Cedar Point Blvd # D, Cedar Point. We have been pleased with the care they have provided. Their phone number is (252) 764-2121. Your rental property information may have a suggested medical number. JCMC, a family/pediatric walk-in practice just opened near Lowe's

Grocery Store in Cape Carteret. Their phone number is 252-424-0004. A neighbor used them recently for her four-year old daughter and was very pleased with the results.

If you have a true emergency, dial 911 and give the folks your location. A few years ago, I almost had a heat stroke, and my wife called the Western Carteret Emergency folks via 911, and they were at our house in minutes. I know the Emerald Isle and other Carteret-based teams are just as efficient.

If you need to go a hospital emergency room, Carteret General Hospital is 21 miles from the Coast Guard Road stoplight. Unless your rental is five miles or more down the beach, my guess is that it is quicker to go by way of Highway 24. Again if it is a serious emergency, get the emergency folks involved, they will get you there quicker. Also Emergency Room personnel respond very quickly to someone arriving in an ambulance.

My wife had surgery in Carteret General, and we were very pleased with the care that she received there. There is a regional medical center in New Bern and an even bigger one in Greenville, but hopefully you won't need any of those services.

One of my neighbors, Dr. Scott, is our personal dentist and runs Crystal Coast Dentistry in Cape Carteret just across the street from PNC Bank. Their phone number is 252 393-8168. If you cannot get an appointment there, another practice is Anderson & Slack in Swansboro. My wife went there before we settled on Dr. Scott's practice. Their phone number is 910 326-3611.

One word of caution should go to the men and boys of the group. If you are planning on getting a haircut while on vacation, remember that we are located very close to a Marine base. That means that a number of barbers in the area default to a military style haircut even when instructed to do otherwise. I have had good luck with Great Clips in Cape Carteret. I even use their smartphone app to check in so I do not have to wait. They have never scalped me. I cannot say about the same thing about some other barbershops in the area.

If need some vehicle repairs while here, I can highly recommend Cedar Point Tire. They will treat you fairly. Their phone number is 252 393-3188. If you look them up on Google Maps, Google has them on the wrong side of the road. They are right beside the pink building, Coastal Outlet. Remember this is a small town area, and people here are very willing to be helpful; so do not be afraid to ask for help or recommendations. Speaking of recommendations, it you need a boat repair while in the area, call Steven Dixon at Dixon Marine. His phone number is 919 738-4178.

If you need a vet while in the area, Brigadoon in Cedar Point is a nearby place to start. Their phone number is 252 393-6581. If you come across the bridge from Emerald Isle, turn left onto Highway 24 and Brigadoon is on the left about seven tenths of a mile after you turn at the stoplight. There are vets in Morehead City with more diagnostic equipment.

We have been pleased with Dr. Roxanne K Taylor, located in Bridges Professional Park at 214 Commerce Ave, Morehead City. Her practice phone number is (252) 247-5595.

Our area has plenty of churches. We only have experience with one, Cape Carteret Presbyterian Church. It is located on Yaupon Drive just down the road on the right after you pass Lowe's Home Improvement on the left heading east on Highway 24 from the stoplight at Route 58. Our church loves to have visitors, and we do not turn away people wearing shorts or dressed casually. Sunday worship starts at 11:00 AM, and once a month, usually the first Sunday, we have a luncheon after the service. There is always plenty of food, and visitors are welcome to join us. You will not have to look hard to find a church in the area. They are all over the place including on Emerald Isle. If you are here in the fall, you can even enjoy some Episcopalian lobsters. We have only missed one year of eating lobsters since we moved down here.

There are plenty of other events and festivals that take place in the area. Aside from reading the hand-lettered sheets, which are often seen posted on the shoulder of the intersection of Highways 24 & 58, you can often find information in the Tideland News, which is a very nice local paper published every Wednesday afternoon. There are free magazines like Carolina Salt and lots of brochures or posters listing events in most of the stores. It was one of those flyers that alerted us the pancake breakfasts that are hosted monthly except for December and January by the Emerald EMS. The next scheduled ones are June 18, July 2, and

August 13 from 7AM until 11AM. You get a couple of huge pancakes, two cakes of sausage and your beverage for a donation of only $5. We enjoyed the one Memorable Day weekend. We heard breakfast at most area restaurants was a long wait. We were served within five minutes.

Speaking of events, if you are interested in hosting a wedding or event in the area, I can recommend Crystal Coast Tent and Event Rentals, LLC. They do a wonderful job. Just ask for Chris Kollar and tell him that David sent you. Their store in Cedar Point also often has cupcakes for sale during part of each Friday.

Also do not forget my friends in the travel bureau who are now located in Emerald Isle on the right just before you get to the BB&T Bank. The tourist bureau is the best place to find out what is happening. While it might be hard to pull out of traffic on check-in day, they are well worth a visit. The staff is very knowledgeable. They have a wealth of information including maps and the latest details about festivals and concerts like the EmeraldFest and SwanFest Concerts that take place all summer. They can also let you have a look at the paperback version of my books. There is another tourist bureau in Swansboro at the corner of South Water and West Church. It is only a short walk from the South end of Front St. but it does not have staff like the one on the island. If you are really stumped stop by Emerald Isle's Town office. The friendly folks there will point you in the right direction.

If you get a chance and would like to go for a boat ride in the Swansboro area, do not forget the Lady Swan. As they say on their website "The Lady Swan departs daily on scheduled cruises to view the natural surroundings and explore the unspoiled beauty of the areas of Swansboro, Hammocks Beach, and Jones Island. This 40' vessel is handicap accessible, and the full shade top, padded seats and onboard restroom will insure comfort during your cruise." We can highly recommend their cruises. I am looking forward to my next visit with them. Their phone number is (910) 325-1200.

A few last thoughts as you are planning your visit. Our beaches stay clean because a lot of people care about them and want them to be around for generations to come. Please haul all your garbage from the beaches and please do not put anything harmful in our waters.

If you have time during your visit drop by North Carolina Coastal Federation's offices at 3609 Highway 24 in Ocean between Cape Carteret and Morehead City. They do oyster bed and wetland restorations. They even restored the wetlands in front our church and the Baptist Church. They sometimes have projects where volunteers can participate. They are planning another shoreline cleanup on June 14, of Jones Island in the White Oak. It is one of several where you can register to be part of the crew.

A Second Helping collects leftover food from vacationers. Collection sites will be located beside Beside Bert's Surf Shop (300 Islander Dr) 8am-11am Corner of Emerald Drive (Hwy 58) & Islander Dr. and at Stir It Up Coffee Shop 6:30am-9am Emerald Plantation (Food Lion). The program will run through Labor Day weekend.

For the most current information on weather, fishing, and excitement, visit my website [crystalcoastlife.com].

I write about the area continually so my posts are a good source of up to date information. There is also a contact form available on my blog. I try to respond to all requests for information that I receive there, but I think you will find most of the information you need in this book.

There are other helpful sources of information. You can even download the official Emerald Isle app by BarZ Adventures at either the App Store or Google Play. You can download a brief PDF Visitor's Guide from the Emerald Isle Town website. It has some useful phone numbers, but I am confident that I have given what you need to have a great vacation. If you add the Kindle version with all the links for the many pictures and detailed information about the area that I have written over the years, you will have enough information to cover almost every facet of a great vacation. You can often get an idea of how things are at the beach by just looking at the many pictures that I post in various places during the month.

This picture is one that I took in 2013 from the Bogue Inlet Pier. It is a few years old but it still captures the spirit of the area.

If my pictures and your time here end up helping you fall in love with the Crystal Coast, I am happy to answer questions about the area so do not hesitate to get in touch with me via the contact form on my blog.

While this is the end of this book, our Kindle version has an appendix with more maps about getting to area. They are printable from your computer. The Kindle version also includes a few favorite recipes, some pictures of feathered friends, some area fish, more great scenery and one of the many Carolina Anoles or greenies as we call them that patrol our gardens.

If you like this book, you might want to try some of our other books like A Taste for the Wild, Canada's Maritimes. The book is about a trip back to New Brunswick where my wife and I had a large cattle farm in the seventies and early eighties. Or if you really want to know why I headed to the coast as quickly as possible, try The Pomme Company, my book about my career of twenty years at Apple.

I still remember well the first time that I visited Emerald Isle. It was probably the summer of 1969 and most of the driving to get to the Point required us to drive down the beach in my old four-wheel drive lime green Bronco. The visit was with my uncle Austin. I still have some great memories from that first trip here. I hope the memories you make on your trip stay with you as long as mine from that first trip have.

Thanks for reading our book. We hope you find our travel guide useful and that your time at our beaches gives you some priceless memories. Please let us know if you see any errors or things that you believe should be included in our next edition. Also if you want more color pictures of the area, do not forget our book, 100 Pictures, 1000 Words, A Crystal Coast Year. It is another Kindle book available for only $2.99. It has the best 100 pictures out of the over 40,000 that I took during 2013. The pictures are specially designed to give you an even better view of the area than the ones in this book. You can also buy individual digital pictures to print and frame from the book for 99 cents.

There is just one more thing as Steve Jobs used to say. The company where I have my day job, WideOpen Networks, hopes that by the summer of 2017, coming to Emerald Isle might be the easiest way to get a taste of our Gigabit fiber networks. A great network might let people stay longer and enjoy our beaches even more. This next picture was taken at the Point by son with his drone before the drone regulations got so tough. It was taken during Thanksgiving 2015 so the beach has a number of fishermen. The beach at the Point is visible and Bear Island is on the horizon. It is a good picture to let burn into your memory.

How to Become a Facebook Friend?

If you want to become a Facebook friend, use the contact form [http://www.crystalcoastlife.com/blog/contact-me/] at my blog to let me know that you want to be friends. Just mention my favorite Great Egret, Frank 29x and I will approve your friendship request.

A Wave to Motivate You

The picture above was taken at Third Street Beach. I live for the time of year when the water takes on those beautiful colors. The final picture on the next page was taken at the true Point, the westernmost piece of sand on Bogue Banks.

David's Map of Favorite Spots for Memories

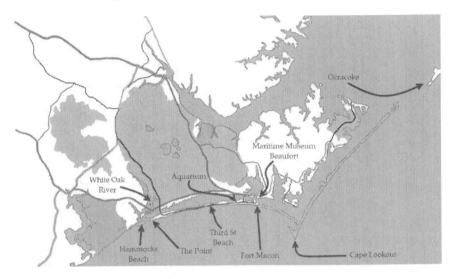

The Point, a great place to make a special memory.

Made in the USA
Middletown, DE
14 June 2016